The Girl's Guide to Winning a NASCAR Driver

The Girl's Guide to Winning a NASCAR Driver

SECRETS TO GRABBING HIS ATTENTION AND STEALING HIS HEART

Liz Allison

CENTER
STREET

NEW YORK   BOSTON   NASHVILLE

Center Street
Hachette Book Group USA
237 Park Avenue
New York, NY 10017
Visit our website at www.centerstreet.com.

Center Street is a division of Hachette Book Group USA, Inc.
The Center Street name and logo is a registered trademark of the Hachette Book Group USA, Inc.
Printed in the United States of America
First edition: September 2007
10 9 8 7 6 5 4 3 2 1

Library of Congress Cataloging-in-Publication Data

Allison, Liz.
    The girl's guide to winning a NASCAR driver : secrets to grabbing his attention and stealing his heart / Liz Allison. — 1st ed.
    p. cm.
    ISBN-13: 978-1-59995-710-4
    ISBN-10: 1-59995-710-8
    1. NASCAR (Association)—Miscellanea. 2. Automobile racing drivers—United States—Miscellanea.
    3. Automobile racing drivers' spouses—United States—Miscellanea. I. Title.

GV1029.9.S74A557 2007
796.72—dc22   2006101317

Illustrations by Lucy Truman

This book is dedicated to all of the **NASCAR** wives
both past and present.
You are the unsung heroes behind the drivers
we all know and love.

Acknowledgments

I am very blessed in the fact that I have a championship-caliber team behind every lap that I turn. A driver is only as good as his team, as this writer is only as good as her team. I am so grateful for the members of my crew, who enable me to do what I love and offer great guidance and support through the process. If not for each one of you, I would be behind the wall before the race even started.

A very special thank-you to my agent, Pamela Harty, who is the best crew chief anyone could ask for. I cannot imagine that I would be where I am today without your great pit strategy and gentle guidance.

Racing with honor and integrity is what makes some teams stand above their competition. A loving thank-you to my attorney, Alden Webb, who radiates both attributes. I am so lucky to have you!

As with any driver, there is always that one person behind the scenes that deserves a gold medal, that someone who goes the extra mile or does not quit when the workday is done. That special someone for me is my editor, Christina Boys, who always goes the extra mile. Thank you for grasping my vision and embracing my passion.

A great sponsor is not only hard to come by but also what makes race teams possible. I am thrilled to have Center Street as my primary sponsor and my publishing home for the *Girl's Guide* series. A big hug and heartfelt thanks to Rolf, Jana, Preston, Meredith, Brynn, Laini, Lori, and Jennette for your hard-charging effort and support.

Racing would not be the same without NASCAR at the helm. An extra-special thanks to Jen White, Mark Dyer, Emily Ross, Kerry Tharp, and Scott

Warfield at NASCAR for your continued support, which means more to me than words can express.

Having a winning pit crew is essential to getting a driver to Victory Lane on any given race day. If not for my crew, I would be lost. Each one of you played a significant role in this book and for that I truly thank you. My pit crew: Donna, Connie, Pandora, Wendy, Russ, Larry Mac, Linda R., Mom, Dad, Grey, Jack, and Linda H.

NASCAR Nextel Cup Series racing owes everything to its fans. If not for the support of the fans, the sport would be lost. I feel the same way about my fans. Thank you for supporting me and embracing my wacky sense of writing. I do what I do because of you.

Each year NASCAR crowns one NASCAR Nextel Cup Series champion, the one driver/team that stands above the rest of the field. I am awarding Ryan, Krista, Robbie, and Bella the champion's trophy. You so unselfishly allow me to chase my dreams. I love each one of you with every ounce of my soul.

CAUTION

NOT FOR THE WEAK OF HEART—

Serious (Kind of)
Competitors Only

Contents

PART FIVE

The Black Flag

PART SIX

The White Flag

PART SEVEN

The Checkered Flag

Introduction

Have you ever caught yourself daydreaming about your favorite NASCAR driver—perhaps even picturing yourself walking down the aisle with a pair of spark plugs in one hand and Carl Edwards in the other? Well, ladies, I hate to break it to you but *you are not alone.*

In May of 2006, *The Girl's Guide to NASCAR* hit the shelves and I was lucky enough to have the opportunity to be interviewed on more than one hundred radio stations. I even traveled to New York for a whirlwind media blitz, which included the *Today* show, *Fox & Friends,* ESPN's *Cold Pizza,* and ESPN News *Hot List.* Wanna guess the number one question I was asked?

You got it . . . HOW DO YOU MARRY A NASCAR DRIVER? Who would have thought that such a technical sport would have so many girls wanting to know how to catch a NASCAR driver by the tail (relatively speaking that is)?

When I met my future husband (way) back in 1988, I found myself wrapped up in his spell from the get-go. What is with these guys that can snatch our hearts with a simple hello? Now, granted, I had no idea this somewhat lanky stranger who had caught my attention was a NASCAR driver.

I have to admit that when I found out he was *the* Davey Allison, NASCAR superstar, I found myself intrigued by his crazy line of work. There is just something about a guy who chooses to drive in circles at 185 mph.

That was the beginning of my fast-paced life right then and there, and I've been turning left ever since that chance meeting at Summerville Speedway.

Ladies, I have to warn you, the life of a driver's wife is certainly not the easiest thing in the world, nor is it the fairy tale everyone thinks it is. I can tell you it is never boring. Traveling the circuit ten months out of the year and trying desperately to maintain some sort of normal family life are just a few of the challenges NASCAR wives faced years ago and still face today.

Okay, do you still want to win a driver's heart?

Could it be as difficult as you think?

Sit back and take notes . . . I will have you race-ready before the checkered flag waves.

Ladies, Start Your Engines!

Part One

⚙

Qualifying

"Are you race-ready?"

Ready, Set, Go~ Not So Fast

Remember the wise old saying *patience is a virtue*? How about *practice makes perfect*? And who could forget that *first impressions are everything*? Let's just say *you cannot run before you walk* when it comes to meeting Mr. Right. So let's start with what every girl needs to know before she heads out the door hoping to steal her favorite driver's heart.

The NASCAR world is very complex and, you guessed it . . . *FAST.* In order to understand a racer, you have to get inside his head. Fasten your seat belts, ladies, and pull the straps tight because this is going to be your crash course in NASCAR racing.

The Top Five . . .
RENEGADES

1. Dale Earnhardt Jr.
2. Paul Menard
3. Martin Truex Jr.
4. Elliott Sadler
5. Tony Stewart

NASCAR: Past, Present, and Future

The National Association for Stock Car Auto Racing has seen many changes over the years and many faces, but only a few have graced the top positions, and one name appears far more than any other. NASCAR has basically always been run by the founding France family.

The Who's Who of NASCAR

Bill France Sr.—A banker turned race car driver from Washington, D.C. France took a far-fetched dream and made it a reality by calling the famous meeting in 1947 at the Streamline Hotel in Daytona Beach, Florida. This meeting of businessmen would change the course of auto racing forever. NASCAR ran its first race on the beaches of Daytona on February 15, 1948. NASCAR became incorporated less than a week later.

Bill France Jr.—Took over the reins when Bill Sr. stepped down in 1972. Bill Jr. charted new territory with the modern era of NASCAR. He retired from his position in November of 2000.

Mike Helton—Succeeded Bill France Jr. as president of NASCAR in a position that he still holds today. Helton is the first (and only to date) non–France family member to sit in the top seat.

Brian France—Bill Jr.'s only son and youngest of the two children. Brian is chairman of the board and chief executive officer of NASCAR.

Lesa France Kennedy—The elder of the two children, she is the president of ISC (International Speedway Corporation), which is a publicly owned company that promotes motorsports events, including Daytona International Speedway.

NASCAR has been able to stay in line with what the motorsports fans of America (and abroad) have wanted for more than fifty years. The sport is healthier now than it has ever been.

The New NASCAR, as we refer to it today, is made up of powerhouse drivers with millions of dollars invested in their driving abilities. NASCAR is the fastest-growing sport in America and could one day soon be waving the green flag for NASCAR Nextel Cup Series events in places like Mexico and Canada.

NASCAR racing leaves many scratching their heads as they wonder what it is about the sport that is so addictive. You got it baby . . . it's the fast cars and the ever so cute drivers. Could you ask for anything more?

fast fact

What we refer to today as the NASCAR Nextel Cup Series has not always carried that name. The sponsoring name has changed several times throughout the years but NASCAR has always been the sanctioning body.

1949–1950—Strictly Stock
1950–1971—Grand National
1971–1986—Winston Cup Grand National Division
1986–2003—Winston Cup Series
2004–Present—Nextel Cup Series*

*Nextel and Sprint merged in 2005, which could result in a name change.

fast fact

- There are an estimated 75 million NASCAR fans.
- Over 40 percent of that fan base is female.
- One of NASCAR's fastest-growing demographics is the young adult female between the ages of eighteen and twenty-five.
- The average age of a NASCAR driver has dropped an estimated ten years since the birth of the New NASCAR (2004).
- More than half of the NASCAR drivers today are SINGLE!

How They Met

PAULA AND STERLING MARLIN

Paula and Sterling are known around the NASCAR Nextel Cup Series as one of the most down-home and fun-natured couples on the circuit. They have been married for almost thirty years and racing has always been the cornerstone of the marriage.

Paula and Sterling have known each other as long as they can remember, but it wasn't until a double date (each with someone else) that they realized their connection. Paula's boyfriend had set his friend Sterling up with her cousin for a double date that didn't exactly go as planned, and opened the door for Sterling and Paula to begin seeing each other. It seems that Paula and Sterling had eyes for each other, something their respective dates did not appreciate!

Paula and Sterling kept crossing each other's path, but it was not until a church hayride that Sterling got up enough nerve to ask Paula for her phone number. One date led to another and before they knew it, they were an item. When Paula graduated from Franklin High School in 1976, she had a brief encounter with a local community college but decided quickly that being with Sterling was all she wanted and that school wouldn't help educate her for life as a racer's wife.

On Christmas Day 1977, Sterling asked Paula's father for her hand in marriage. The young couple were married the following July in front of friends and family.

Driver Mentality

Driver vs. Joe Average

	Driver	Joe Average
Average speed	180 mph	75 mph
Monday morning routine	Sleeps late	Punches the clock at 8:00 A.M.
Prefers turning	Left	Whichever way the road leads
Earns	A million or so a year	Lives paycheck to paycheck
Sunday meals	One	Three and lots of snacks
Has car serviced in	Fifteen seconds	Forty-five minutes at best
Receives marriage proposals	Once a week	Maybe once in a lifetime

fast fact

The HANS device is a mandatory collar-style piece of safety equipment using straps that connect to the helmet to keep the driver's head from snapping back and forth (think whiplash) in a wreck.

Okay, so now that we've covered the roots of the NASCAR world, do you dare step inside the head of a racer? You only had to tighten your seat belt before—now it's time to get the HANS device on, girls! Race car drivers always have one thing on their minds—racing. The best way to grab a driver's heart is to (try to) understand that the *need for speed* is much greater than what you and I can fathom.

So, what could make a relatively normal human being want to strap into a hot race car, in a small compartment, and beat and bang with the neighbors at high speeds for hours on end just to go to a place called . . . VICTORY LANE? Sound reasonable? Not for most of us sane people.

Race car drivers are similar in their drive and passion to fighter pilots. Most drivers will tell you that even though they know they are in a dangerous profession, the danger factor rarely enters their minds. In fact, some drivers believe that if danger or fear becomes a factor, they should consider hanging up the helmet for good. It is the opinion of many that the best racers in the world respect danger but are not fearful of what could be looming around the corner.

Maybe it is because most of the guys have been racing since they could walk. Did you know the average age of a driver when he started racing is eight . . . EIGHT YEARS OLD mind you. What happened to playing with lizards and watching *Pokémon*?

Racing is a unique sport in that most kids discover their interest in racing very early in their lives due to a parent's or other family member's desire to race. Little shop brats usually grow up to be big shop brats. Very few venture away from what becomes a way of life. Few racers come into the sport's top level without being raised in and around race cars. So, is racing passed down from generation to generation? You betcha!

The Top Five . . .

WAYS DRIVERS' WIVES KEEP FEAR OUT OF THEIR MINDS DURING A RACE

1. Eat chocolate.
2. Go for a stroll around the paddock area.
3. Give the dog a bath.
4. Read a great book.
5. Chat with other wives.

You Know He's a NASCAR Driver If He . . .

1. Writes your phone number down on track notes from Daytona.
2. Picks you up for a date in his #8 Budweiser Chevy.
3. Pulled out a Sharpie to sign his credit card slip after dinner.
4. When the champagne arrives to celebrate your anniversary, he climbs on the table to thank his sponsors.
5. Invited you to his place to watch reruns of last weekend's race.

Ladies . . . Start Your Engines

O kay girls, I know what you're thinking . . . boys . . . boys . . . boys! Yes, that's right, lots of cute boys in uniform driving *extremely fast*.

Good heavens, what is there not to love about race car drivers? You can look deep into the "greatest romances of all time" archives and find that men in uniform have *always* been able to catch the ladies' eyes. And it sure doesn't hurt that these guys are risk-takers.

So what is it about race car drivers that has millions of women hot on their trails? Let's just say when you have a good-looking, *single*, successful, adventuresome, well-spoken guy who—oh yeah by the way—just happens to be a NASCAR driver . . . what's not to love?

But have you ever wondered *why* there are so many more young drivers in the NASCAR Nextel Cup Series than in years past? The majority of the drivers today started racing go-karts between the ages of four and six. This is a far cry from drivers in years past. It used to be the racers started catching the racing bug in their teen years versus the drivers of today who learn to race before they learn to ride a bike. Most drivers start out in go-karts, then move to Bandeleros or Allison Legacy cars. From there the drivers take many different routes, but most choose Late Models at their local race track.

The average age of a NASCAR driver has dropped considerably in the last five years. What used to be the average age of thirty-five is now twenty-five. So how does that affect the driver's marital status? You got it, more *SINGLE drivers!*

Think about it . . . how many people do you know with successful careers at the age of twenty-five who really have time for a personal life? Probably not many. Most successful athletes are busy honing their skills instead of starting families.

Over half of the field of NASCAR drivers are currently not spoken for. *Ooh la la!* The lineup of single NASCAR drivers is like going to a fresh flower market . . . lots of pretties to look at and lots to choose from. So where is a gal to begin?

The Finding Mr. Right Quiz

- Take the quiz
- Tally your score
- Find your Mr. Right

1. **What is your ideal date?**
   A. A casual meal and movie
   B. Staying at home for a little takeout and a rented movie
   C. A candlelight dinner and walk on the beach
   D. Club hopping all night
   E. Going to a NASCAR race, of course!

2. **What is the best date movie?**
   A. *Sleepless in Seattle*
   B. *The Ring*
   C. *Pretty Woman*
   D. *Meet the Parents*
   E. *Talladaga Nights*

3. **What trait is most important in your Mr. Right?**
   A. Sense of humor
   B. Self-confidence
   C. Sincerity
   D. Assertiveness
   E. Ability to drive—*fast*

4. **What best suits your style?**
   A. Outdoorsy
   B. Adventuresome
   C. Boy-next-door
   D. James Dean
   E. Hard-charging

5. **Best Place for a Honeymoon**
   A. Hawaii
   B. Colorado mountains
   C. The French Alps
   D. Myrtle Beach
   E. Any track where NASCAR races

6. **Favorite Pastime**
   A. Golf
   B. Fishing
   C. Boating
   D. Video games
   E. Racing anything with wheels

Answer Key

Add up your score to see who best suits you. If you answered mostly:

> As—Elliott Sadler, Brian Vickers, David Stremme
>
> Bs—Tony Stewart, Martin Truex Jr., Paul Menard, Carl Edwards
>
> Cs—Kasey Kahne, Greg Biffle, Clint Bowyer, Robby Gordon, Casey Mears, Reed Sorenson, Jon Wood
>
> Ds—Kyle Busch, Dale Earnhardt Jr., Denny Hamlin, Jamie McMurray
>
> Es—All of them!

How They Met

KIM AND JEFF BURTON

Kim and Jeff met when Kim was only fourteen years old and Jeff only fifteen. Jeff was the passenger in a car that was riding by a young attractive girl on her bike when he decided to yell out at her. He later told one of his friends about the girl that he was destined to meet. His friend not only knew who the mysterious girl was, but also knew her phone number.

It did not take Jeff long to get up the nerve to call Kimberle Brown, a call that lasted for two hours. The two made plans to meet at a football game that weekend. As planned, Kim and her friends waited at the football game for the mystery guy she told her friends all about.

However, the meeting did not go quite as planned when the brakes on Jeff's bike suddenly decided not to work. Jeff (not so graciously) plowed into Kim and her group of friends. Kim found herself totally amazed that somehow this guy managed to crash into them but never missed a beat. He just hopped off his bike and kept on talking.

Their budding romance turned into weekend movies and long phone conversations all the way until high school, when the two decided to give the relationship a break. After only three months, the couple decided they were much better together than apart and have been together ever since. Kim and Jeff were married in South Boston on February 1, 1992, just a few blocks from where they met as kids.

The Starting Lineup— "Ooh La La"

Now it's time to get to know all about your favorite guy!

Date of birth: December 23, 1969
Hometown: Vancouver, Washington
Resides: Mooresville, North Carolina
Height: 5'9"
Weight: 170 pounds
Hair color: Brown
Hobbies: Flying/piloting, boating
Favorite charities: Speedway Children's Charity, Greg Biffle Foundation, Victory Junction Gang Camp
Web site: gregbiffle.com
Fan club: gregbiffle.com
First NASCAR Nextel Cup Series start: California—April 28, 2002

ZODIAC SIGN: **Capricorn**
Practical, ambitious, disciplined, patient, careful, humorous, reserved, grudging, pessimistic

Girlfriend to Girlfriend

Now that Greg Biffle (finally) popped the question to his longtime girlfriend Nicole Lunders, he's on the Endangered Single Drivers list. But not to worry, there are still lots of single guys to choose from!

Likes: Reliability, professionalism, firm foundations, purpose
Dislikes: Wild schemes, ridiculing, fantasies, jobs without purpose
Love match: Taurus, Cancer, Virgo, Scorpio, Capricorn, Pisces

WHAT YOU NEED TO KNOW

- Discovered in 1995 by Benny Parsons (TNT NASCAR analyst) while running the NASCAR Winter Heat Series
- Referred to as "the Biff"
- 1998 NASCAR Craftsman Truck Series Rookie of the Year
- Captured nine checkered flags in the 1999 NASCAR Craftsman Truck Series
- 2000 NASCAR Craftsman Truck Series champion
- 2001 NASCAR Busch Series Rookie of the Year
- 2002 NASCAR Busch Series champion
- 2005 NASCAR Nextel Cup Series winningest driver

CLINT BOWYER

Date of birth: May 30, 1979
Hometown: Emporia, Kansas
Resides: Welcome, North Carolina
Height: 5'11"
Weight: 180 pounds
Hair color: Blond
Hobbies: Old cars, lake life and boating
Favorite charity: American Cancer Society
Web site: clintbowyer.com
Fan club: clintbowyer.com
First NASCAR Nextel Cup Series start: Phoenix—April 23, 2005

ZODIAC SIGN: **Gemini**

Adaptable, versatile, communicative, witty, intellectual, eloquent, youthful, lively, nervous, intense, cunning, inquisitive, inconsistent

Likes: Talking, variety, multiple projects, reading, unusual things

The Top Five . . .

DRIVER GOALS

1. Winning the NASCAR Nextel Cup championship.
2. Winning their second NASCAR Nextel Cup championship.
3. Beating Richard Petty's winning record (200 wins).
4. Passing Jeff Gordon in total race earnings.
5. Beating Jimmie Johnson at Lowe's Motor Speedway.

Dislikes: Feeling tied down, school, being alone, being in a rut, dead-end situations

Love match: Aries, Aquarius, Leo, Libra, Sagittarius

WHAT YOU NEED TO KNOW

- Started racing at age five
- Won over 200 motocross races between the ages of five and twelve
- 2000 Modified champion at Thunderhill Speedway
- 2001 Modified champion at Lakeside Speedway and Heartland Park
- 2002 Modified champion at Lakeside Speedway, Late Models champion at 1-70 Speedway, NASCAR Weekly Racing Series Midwest champion
- Moved to NASCAR's AutoZone Elite Division—Midwest Series
- 2003—Discovered by car owner Richard Childress at Nashville Super-speedway
- 2004—Shared NASCAR Busch Series driver duties with Kevin Harvick for Richard Childress Racing
- 2005—Finished second in overall point standings in the NASCAR Busch Series for Childress Racing
- 2006—Moved to NASCAR Nextel Cup Series racing for Childress Racing

KYLE BUSCH

The Top Five...

MOST LIKELY FAMILY MEN

1. Greg Biffle
2. Kyle Busch
3. Denny Hamlin
4. Reed Sorenson
5. David Stremme

Date of birth: May 2, 1985

Hometown: Las Vegas, Nevada

Resides: Concord, North Carolina

Height: 6'1"

Weight: 160 pounds

Hair color: Brown

Hobbies: Video games

Favorite charity: Hendrick Marrow Foundation

Web site: nascar.com/drivers/dps/kbusch01/cup/index. html

Fan club: Kyle Busch Fan Club, PO Box 1225, Harrisburg, NC 28075

First NASCAR Nextel Cup Series start: Las Vegas—March 7, 2004

Zodiac Sign: **Taurus**

Patient, reliable, warmhearted, loving, persistent, determined, placid, jealous, possessive, self-indulgent, resentful, greedy

Likes: Stability, downtime, being comfortable

Dislikes: Being rushed, disruption, pushy people or situations, being cooped up

Love match: Cancer, Virgo, Scorpio, Capricorn, Pisces

What you need to know

- Younger brother of 2004 NASCAR Nextel Cup Series champion Kurt Busch
- Started racing go-karts at age six
- In 1999, won more than sixty-five races in Legends cars
- At age sixteen made NASCAR Craftsman Truck Series debut
- Raced full American Speed Association (ASA) circuit while still in high school
- Graduated with honors in 2002 (one year early) from Durango High School in Las Vegas
- Signed development deal with Hendrick Motorsports in February 2003
- 2004 NASCAR Busch Series Rookie of the Year at age nineteen
- 2005—Named replacement driver for retiring Terry Labonte
- Became the series's youngest winner at the age of twenty, September 2005, at California Speedway
- 2005 NASCAR Nextel Cup Series Rookie of the Year at age twenty
- Favorite TV shows: *Desperate Housewives* and *Grey's Anatomy*

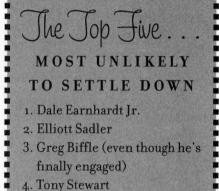

The Top Five . . .

MOST UNLIKELY TO SETTLE DOWN

1. Dale Earnhardt Jr.
2. Elliott Sadler
3. Greg Biffle (even though he's finally engaged)
4. Tony Stewart
5. Jamie McMurray

DALE EARNHARDT JR.

Date of birth: October 10, 1974

Hometown: Kannapolis, North Carolina

Resides: Mooresville, North Carolina

Height: 6'0"
Weight: 165 pounds
Hair color: Blond
Hobbies: car restoration, video games, computers, music
Favorite charity: Victory Junction Gang Camp
Web site: dalejr.com
Fan club: Club E Jr., PO Box 5190, Concord, NC 28027
First NASCAR Nextel Cup Series start: Charlotte (Lowe's)—May 30, 1999

ZODIAC SIGN: **Libra**

Charming, romantic at heart, idealistic, peacemaker, sociable, easygoing, diplomatic, easily influenced, self-indulgent, flirtatious, indecisive
Likes: Gentleness, sharing, nice things, honesty
Dislikes: Violence, fashion police, injustice, dishonesty
Love match: Aries, Gemini, Leo, Sagittarius, Aquarius

WHAT YOU NEED TO KNOW

- Son of legendary racer Dale Earnhardt Sr.
- Grandson of Ralph Earnhardt, also a legendary racer
- Referred to as either "Jr." or "Little E" (Note: Dale Jr. does not like to be called Little E)
- Began racing at age seventeen
- Used the NASCAR Street Stock Division and NASCAR Late Model Stock Division at Concord Motorsport Park to cut his teeth
- Made first NASCAR Busch Series start at Myrtle Beach, South Carolina, in 1997
- 1998 and 1999 NASCAR Busch Series champion
- Loves Frosted Flakes cereal
- Counts Tony Stewart, Martin Truex Jr., and Elliott Sadler as his closest racing friends

CARL EDWARDS

Date of birth: August 15, 1979
Hometown: Columbia, Missouri
Resides: Mooresville, North Carolina
Height: 6'1"

Weight: 185 pounds

Hair color: Dirty blond

Hobbies: Racing, mountain-biking, working out

Favorite charity: Boone County Sheriffs Department, Columbia Police Department

Web site: carledwards.com

Fan club: carledwards.com

First NASCAR Nextel Cup Series start: Michigan— August 22, 2004

ZODIAC SIGN: **Leo**

Generous, creative, enthusiastic, faithful, broad-minded, patronizing, bossy, intolerant, interfering, pompous

Likes: The finer things in life, drama, children, lavish vacations

Dislikes: Ordinary things, small-minded people, mean people, counting pennies

Love match: Aries, Gemini, Libra, Sagittarius, Aquarius

WHAT YOU NEED TO KNOW

- Referred to as "Flipper"
- Does a back flip when he wins a race
- Father Mike Edwards accumulated over 200 wins spanning four decades in modified stock cars and USAC midgets
- Began racing at age thirteen in Mini Sprints
- From 1994 to 1996 accumulated over fifteen wins in the Mini Sprint series
- 1998 IMCA Modified Rookie of the Year at the Missouri Capital Speedway
- 2000 NASCAR Weekly Racing Series Pro-Modified Division Rookie of the Year and Capital Speedway track champion
- 2002—raced in USAC and NASCAR Craftsman Truck Series
- 2002 Baby Grand National champion
- 2003—signed with Jack Roush to drive full-time in the NASCAR Craftsman Truck Series
- 2003 NASCAR Craftsman Series Rookie of the Year
- August 2004—got the call to replace Jeff Burton in the NASCAR Nextel Cup Series
- 2005 NASCAR Busch Series Rookie of the Year
- Serves as a part-time sheriff's deputy in Columbia

> ## The Top Five . . .
> ### BEST BODS
> 1. Carl Edwards
> 2. Casey Mears
> 3. Reed Sorenson
> 4. Dale Earnhardt Jr.
> 5. Paul Menard

Did You Know. . .

The most athletic of the group is Carl Edwards, who graced the cover of *Men's Health* magazine in 2006.

ROBBY GORDON

Date of birth: January 2, 1969
Hometown: Cerritos, California
Resides: Cornelius, North Carolina
Height: 5'10"
Weight: 180 pounds
Hair color: Brown
Hobbies: Racing anything with wheels, boating, mountain-biking, water-skiing
Favorite charity: Meals on Wheels (makes deliveries himself)
Web site: robbygordon.com
Fan club: robbygordon.com
First NASCAR Nextel Cup Series start: Daytona—February 17, 1991

ZODIAC SIGN: **Capricorn**

Practical, ambitious, disciplined, humorous, grudging, pessimistic
Likes: Reliable people, professionalism, solid foundations, having purpose
Dislikes: Fantasies, wild schemes, jobs without purpose, sarcastic people
Love match: Taurus, Cancer, Virgo, Scorpio, Pisces

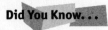

Did You Know...

The most picked favorite color of race car drivers is black.

WHAT YOU NEED TO KNOW

- Started racing motorbikes at age eight
- Started racing cars at sixteen
- Off-road champion six times
- Moved to sport cars in 1990
- Won five GTO races in 1991
- Won in 1992 Trans Am series
- Jumped to open wheels in 1993 and signed with A. J. Foyt
- CART race winner
- IROC winner
- Made jump to NASCAR Cup Series racing in 1991
- 2001—signed with Richard Childress Racing
- Competed in Indianapolis 500 and the Coca-Cola 600 on the same day
- Raced in the famous Baja, and Spain's Rally Car Race of Champions
- 2005—first American to win a stage of the Dakar Rally, a grueling motorsports event, which starts in Portugal and ends in Africa

DENNY HAMLIN

Date of birth: November 18, 1980
Hometown: Chesterfield, Virginia
Resides: Davidson, North Carolina
Height: 6'0"
Weight: 170 pounds
Hair color: Brown
Hobbies: Online racing, video games
Web site: dennyhamlin.com
Fan club: dennyhamlin.com
First NASCAR Nextel Cup Series start: Kansas—
October 9, 2005

ZODIAC SIGN: **Scorpio**
Forceful, determined, emotional, intuitive, exciting, magnetic, powerful, jealous, resentful, secretive, obstinate, compulsive
Likes: Work with a purpose, making a difference, being involved, truthfulness
Dislikes: Demeaning jobs, dishonesty, dead-end relationships, being taken advantage of
Love match: Taurus, Cancer, Virgo, Capricorn, Pisces

WHAT YOU NEED TO KNOW
- Started racing at seven years old
- Earned 127 feature wins in Dirt Karts
- In 2004, made NASCAR Craftsman Truck and Busch Series starts
- Raced full NASCAR Busch Series schedule in 2005
- Began full-time NASCAR Nextel Cup Series career in 2006 with Joe Gibbs Racing
- Won 2006 Budweiser Shootout in Daytona
- 2006 NASCAR Nextel Cup Series Rookie of the Year

Girlfriend to Girlfriend

There are a few single drivers racing in NASCAR Nextel Cup Series that have never shown up with a girl to drivers' intro. That does not mean they have not invited girls to attend a race . . . it only means the ladies were not invited to the more highly visible part of the race day activities. Hmmm!

KASEY KAHNE

Date of birth: April 10, 1980
Hometown: Enumclaw, Washington
Resides: Huntersville, North Carolina
Height: 5'8"
Weight: 150 pounds
Hair color: Brown
Hobbies: Snowmobiling, racing
Favorite charity: Kasey Kahne Foundation
Web site: kaseykahne.com
Fan club: Kasey Kahne Fan Club, 10 West Market Street, Suite 1026, Indianapolis, IN 46205
First NASCAR Nextel Cup Series start: Daytona—February 15, 2004

Zodiac Sign: **Aries**
Adventurous, energetic, pioneering, courageous, dynamic, quick-witted, selfish, quick-tempered, daredevil, impulsive, impatient
Likes: Action, coming in first, challenges, spontaneity, meaningful things
Dislikes: Waiting around, other people's advice, losing
Love match: Gemini, Leo, Libra, Sagittarius, Aquarius

WHAT YOU NEED TO KNOW
- 2000 USAC Midget Series champion
- 2000 Silver Crown Rookie of the Year
- Signed with Ray Evernham and Evernham Motorsports in 2004 to replace the retiring Bill Elliott
- 2004 NASCAR Nextel Cup Series Rookie of the Year
- Close friends with Tony Stewart
- Won first NASCAR Nextel Cup Series race in 2005 at Richmond

JAMIE MCMURRAY

Date of birth: June 3, 1976
Hometown: Joplin, Missouri

Resides: Concord, North Carolina
Height: 5'8"
Weight: 150 pounds
Hair color: Dirty blond
Hobbies: Racing, radio-controlled cars
Favorite charity: Autism Society of America
Web site: jamiemcmurray.com
Fan club: Jamie McMurray Fan Club, PO Box 5034, Concord, NC 28027
First NASCAR Nextel Cup Series start: Talladega—October 6, 2002

ZODIAC SIGN: **Gemini**

Adaptable, versatile, witty, intellectual, youthful, lively, nervous, intense, inquisitive, inconsistent
Likes: Talking, variety, multiple things at once, unusual things
Dislikes: Boring people, talkative people, feeling tied down, school, being alone, dead-end situations
Love match: Aries, Aquarius, Leo, Libra, Sagittarius

WHAT YOU NEED TO KNOW

- Started racing go-karts at age eight
- 1991 World Go-Karting champion
- Made the jump to NASCAR Late Models in 1992
- From 1998 to 1999, raced in RE/MAX Challenge Series
- Debuted in 1999 in the NASCAR Craftsman Truck Series
- Advanced to NASCAR Busch Series in 2001
- Won first NASCAR Nextel Cup Series race in only his second start in October 2002 while filling in for injured veteran driver Sterling Marlin
- Signed on as a full-time NASCAR Nextel Cup Series driver with Chip Ganassi Racing for the 2003 season
- 2003 NASCAR Nextel Cup Series Rookie of the Year
- Raced his first full-time NASCAR Nextel Cup Series season in 2006 as a Roush Racing driver
- Spokesperson for the Autism Society of America

CASEY MEARS

Date of birth: March 12, 1978
Hometown: Bakersfield, California
Resides: Mooresville, North Carolina
Height: 5'8"
Weight: 158 pounds
Hair color: Dark brown
Hobbies: Snowboarding, wakeboarding
Web site: caseymears.com
Fan club: caseymears.com
First NASCAR Nextel Cup Series start: Daytona—February 16, 2003

ZODIAC SIGN: **Pisces**
Sensitive, generous, imaginative, sympathetic, caring, kind-natured, weak, secretive, follows easily, idealistic
Likes: Daydreaming, imagining, getting lost, mysteries
Dislikes: To-do lists, know-it-alls, criticism, being misled
Love match: Taurus, Cancer, Virgo, Scorpio, Capricorn

WHAT YOU NEED TO KNOW
- Son of off-road racer Roger Mears
- Nephew of Indy Car legend Rick Mears
- Started racing BMX Bicycles at age four
- Cut teeth in many different series including go-karts, Superlites Off Road, USAC Triple Crown
- 1995 USAC Triple Crown champion
- From 1996 to 2000, competed in Indy Lights Series
- Competed in the Indy Racing League and CART series from 2000 to 2001
- In 2002, made the full-time jump to NASCAR Busch Series competition
- Signed on to drive full-time in the NASCAR Nextel Cup Series in 2003 with Chip Ganassi Racing
- 2006—first year under a multiyear agreement with Hendrick Motorsports, replacing Brian Vickers

PAUL MENARD

Date of birth: August 21, 1980
Hometown: Eau Claire, Wisconsin
Resides: Mooresville, North Carolina
Height: 5'10"
Weight: 180 pounds
Hair color: Brown
Hobbies: Basketball, ice racing, rescuing greyhounds
Web site: menardsracing.com
Fan club: menardsracing.com
First NASCAR Nextel Cup Series start: Watkins Glen—August 10, 2003

ZODIAC SIGN: **Leo**
Warmhearted, creative, faithful, loving, generous, bossy, intolerant, patronizing
Likes: Nice things, children, animals, drama, action, honesty
Dislikes: Dishonesty, ordinary things, closed-minded people, penny-pinching
Love match: Aries, Gemini, Libra, Sagittarius, Aquarius

WHAT YOU NEED TO KNOW
- From 2000 to 2002, raced ARCA/RE MAX Challenge Series and SCCA Trans Am Series
- Competed in all of NASCAR Top Three Series and ARCA Series events for Andy Petree Racing in 2003
- Joined Dale Earnhardt Inc. as a full-time driver in the NASCAR Busch Series in 2005
- Won first NASCAR Busch Series event at the Milwaukee Mile in 2006
- Signed an agreement with DEI to run the full NASCAR Nextel Cup Series circuit in 2007

ELLIOTT SADLER

Date of birth: April 30, 1975
Hometown: Emporia, Virginia

Resides: Emporia, Virginia
Height: 6'2"
Weight: 195 pounds
Hair color: Brown
Hobbies: Golf, hunting, basketball, water sports
Favorite charity: Victory Junction Gang Camp
Web site: elliottsadler.com
Fan club: Elliott Sadler Fan Club, PO Box 32, Emporia, VA 23847
First NASCAR Nextel Cups Series start: Charlotte (Lowe's)—May 24, 1998

ZODIAC SIGN: **Taurus**

Reliable, determined, warmhearted, funny, patient, loving, possessive, jealous, greedy, resentful

Likes: Downtime, being comfortable in situations, stability, kind people, nature

Dislikes: Being cooped up, disruption, being rushed, forceful people

Love match: Cancer, Virgo, Scorpio, Capricorn, Pisces

WHAT YOU NEED TO KNOW

- Started racing go-karts at age seven
- Captured over 200 wins before jumping to Late Models in his teenage years
- At eighteen, became the 1995 South Boston Speedway track champion
- Was discovered by NASCAR Busch Series car owner Gary Bechtel
- Entered NASCAR Busch Series full-time in 1997
- In 1999, signed on with legendary Wood Brothers Racing to drive full-time in NASCAR Nextel Cup Series
- Captured first Cup Series win in 2001 at Bristol Motor Speedway
- Moved to Robert Yates Racing in 2003
- In 2006, moved to Evernham Motorsports, replacing Jeremy Mayfield
- Loves *Seinfeld* reruns

REED SORENSON

Date of birth: February 5, 1986
Hometown: Peachtree, Georgia
Resides: Concord, North Carolina
Height: 5'10"

Weight: 165 pounds
Hair color: Brown
Hobbies: Weightlifting, video games, water sports
Web site: reedsorenson.com
Fan club: reedsorenson.com
First NASCAR Nextel Cup Series start: Atlanta—October 30, 2005

Zodiac Sign: **Aquarius**

Friendly, honest, inventive, independent, intellectual, spirited thinker, unpredictable, spontaneous, unemotional, flippant

Likes: Daydreaming, having fun, kicking back, planning for the future, good causes

Dislikes: People without a cause, ordinary things, endless promises

Love match: Aries, Gemini, Leo, Libra, Sagittarius

What you need to know

- Started racing Quarter Midgets at age six
- 1997 Quarter Midgets National Champion
- Captured over 250 wins and fifteen different track titles while racing Quarter Midgets
- Racked up eighty-four wins in five full seasons in the Legends Series
- 2003 American Speed Association (ASA) Rookie of the Year at age seventeen, the youngest driver ever
- Made the jump to the NASCAR Busch Series full-time in 2005
- Captured two wins and twelve top fives in his rookie year in the Busch Series
- In 2006, signed on to drive full-time in the NASCAR Nextel Cup Series with Ganassi Racing

TONY STEWART

Date of birth: March 20, 1971
Hometown: Rushville, Indiana
Resides: Columbus, Indiana
Height: 5'9"
Weight: 170 pounds
Hair color: Brown

Hobbies: Bowling, boating, fishing

Favorite charity: Victory Junction Gang Camp

Web site: tonystewart.com

Fan club: Tony Stewart Fan Club, 5671 West 74th Street, Indianapolis, IN 46278

First NASCAR Nextel Cup Series start: Daytona— February 14, 1999

ZODIAC SIGN: **Pisces**

Sensitive, loving, sympathetic, warmhearted, compassionate, imaginative, secretive, wishy-washy, turbulent, harsh

Likes: Getting lost, daydreaming, solitude, mysteries

Dislikes: Being criticized, know-it-alls, to-do lists

Love match: Taurus, Cancer, Virgo, Scorpio, Capricorn

WHAT YOU NEED TO KNOW

- Started racing go-karts at age seven
- 1980 4-cycle Rookie Junior Class champion at Columbus Fairgrounds at age eight
- 1983 International Karting Federation Grand National champion
- 1987 World Karting Association national champion
- Moved to open wheels (Indy Racing League) in 1989
- 1991 USAC Three Quarter Midget Rookie of the Year
- 1994 USAC champion
- 1995 USAC Triple Crown champion (won the National Midget, Sprint, and Silver Crown titles all in one year)
- 1996 IndyCar Series Rookie of the Year
- 1997 IndyCar champion
- Ran a limited NASCAR Busch Series schedule in 1998 for Joe Gibbs Racing
- Signed on with Joe Gibbs in 1999 for a full-time ride in the NASCAR Nextel Cup Series
- 1999 NASCAR Nextel Cup Rookie of the Year
- 2001 World of Outlaws champion car owner
- Owns several USAC teams and four championships
- 2002 NASCAR Nextel Cup Series champion
- 2005 NASCAR Nextel Cup Series champion

- Donated more than $2 million to the Victory Junction Gang Camp
- Loves chocolate ice cream
- Nicknamed "Smoke"

DAVID STREMME

Date of birth: June 19, 1977
Hometown: South Bend, Indiana
Resides: Davidson, North Carolina
Height: 5'11"
Weight: 175 pounds
Hair color: Brown
Hobbies: Inline skating, snowmobiling, mountain-biking
Favorite charity: St. Jude's Hospital
Web site: davidstremme.com
Fan club: davidstremme.com
First NASCAR Nextel Cup Series start: Chicagoland—July 10, 2005

ZODIAC SIGN: **Gemini**
Adaptable, intellectual, youthful, lively, witty, communicative, fun-loving, nervous, inconsistent, intense
Likes: Talking, variety, multiple projects at once, reading, animals
Dislikes: Excessive talkers, feeling tied down, being alone, pushy people, being in a rut
Love match: Aries, Aquarius, Libra, Sagittarius, Leo

WHAT YOU NEED TO KNOW
- Started racing Big Wheels at age six
- Mother, Cindy, and father, Lou, raced in the Midwest
- First victory came in a Big Wheel at the same track his mother and father raced
- Worked in his father's race shop as a kid
- Jumped to the Street Stock Division in 1993
- First win came at age fifteen in his mother's Street Stock car at New Paris Speedway, but officials made him quit until he was of age
- From 1993 to 1997, captured twenty-four wins, two Rookie of the Year titles, and two track championships

- Moved to the NASCAR Late Model Series in 1998
- Raced numerous series, including Open Wheel Modifieds and CRA Super Series
- In 2002, signed on to drive the full American Speed Association (ASA) schedule
- 2002 ASA Rookie of the Year
- 2003 NASCAR Busch Series Rookie of the Year
- Signed on as a full-time NASCAR Nextel Cup Series driver in 2006 for Ganassi Racing

MARTIN TRUEX JR.

The Top Five . . .
BEST BACKSIDES
1. Carl Edwards
2. Dale Earnhardt Jr.
3. Martin Truex Jr.
4. Kasey Kahne
5. Casey Mears

Date of birth: June 29, 1980
Hometown: Mayetta, New Jersey
Resides: Mooresville, North Carolina
Height: 5'11"
Weight: 180 pounds
Hair color: Brown
Hobbies: Video games, fishing, hunting, snowmobiling, four-wheeling
Web site: martintruexjr.com
Fan club: martintruexjr.com
First NASCAR Nextel Cup Series start: Atlanta—October 31, 2004

ZODIAC SIGN: **Cancer**

Emotional, cautious, imaginative, intuitive, clear-thinking, protective, sympathetic, moody, overemotional, clingy, touchy
Likes: Hobbies, being outside, children, parties, romance, country living
Dislikes: Failure, being told what to do, advice, losing
Love Match: Taurus, Virgo, Scorpio, Capricorn, Pisces

WHAT YOU NEED TO KNOW
- Started racing go-karts at age eleven
- 1993 New Egypt Speedway Junior Class champion
- 1994 New Egypt Speedway New Jersey Series champion

- Jumped to Modifieds in 1998 at age eighteen
- Won prestigious Wall Stadium Turkey Derby in 1999, a race that was previously won by his father
- In 2000, jumped to NASCAR Busch North Series
- Won three track records in 2002 while racing the full-time NASCAR Busch North Series
- Signed to drive full-time in the NASCAR Busch Series in 2004 for Dale Earnhardt Jr. and Earnhardt's stepmother, Teresa
- 2004 NASCAR Busch Series champion
- 2005 NASCAR Busch Series champion
- In 2006, signed on as full-time driver for DEI in the NASCAR Nextel Cup Series

BRIAN VICKERS

Date of birth: October 24, 1983
Hometown: Thomasville, North Carolina
Resides: Thomasville, North Carolina
Height: 5'11"
Weight: 160 pounds
Hair color: Dirty blond
Hobbies: Golf, video games
Favorite charity: Victory Junction Gang Camp, Hendrick Marrow Foundation, and Phantom University Junior Challenge
Web site: brianvickers.com
Fan club: Brian Vickers Fan Club, 27 High Tech Boulevard, Thomasville, NC 27360
First NASCAR Nextel Cup Series start: Charlotte (Lowe's)—October 11, 2003

ZODIAC SIGN: **Scorpio**
Determined, forceful, powerful, magnetic, intuitive, emotional, resentful, jealous, secretive
Likes: Charitable causes, getting involved, persuasive people, truth
Dislikes: Dead-end relationships, demeaning jobs, purposeless work, being taken advantage of
Love match: Taurus, Cancer, Virgo, Capricorn, Pisces

What you need to know

- Started racing yard karts at the age of eight
- In 1998, won five races in the only year of Allison Legacy car competition
- In 1999, won six races and eleven pole positions in NASCAR's weekly southeastern racing series Late Models Stock Division
- MotorSport magazine voted him "Rising Star of the Year" in 1999
- Won two races in USAR ProCup series in 2000
- Made first Busch Series start in July 2001 at age seventeen
- Graduated from Trinity High School in North Carolina with honors in May 2002
- Skipped his senior prom to race at Bristol in the Busch Series
- Handpicked by the late Ricky Hendrick to drive a Hendrick Motorsports Busch Series entry
- 2003 Busch Series champion in his first full season at the age of twenty
- Competed for NASCAR Nextel Series Cup Rookie of the Year honors in 2004

JON WOOD

Date of birth: October 25, 1981
Hometown: Stuart, Virginia
Resides: Mooresville, North Carolina
Height: 5'10"
Weight: 145 pounds
Hair color: Blond
Hobbies: Golf, radio-controlled airplanes
Web site: woodbrothersracing.com
Fan club: woodbrothersracing.com
First NASCAR Nextel Cup Series start: Las Vegas Motor Speedway—March 11, 2007

ZODIAC SIGN: **Scorpio**

Determined, powerful, magnetic, intuitive, emotional, resentful, jealous, compulsive

Likes: Playing a part in a good cause, dry humor, honest people, family time

Dislikes: Meaningless relationships, worrisome people, saying no, dishonesty
Love match: Taurus, Cancer, Virgo, Capricorn, Pisces

WHAT YOU NEED TO KNOW

- Grandson of the legendary car owner Glen Wood, who helped form Wood Brothers Racing over fifty years ago, and which is one of the longest-running Cup Series teams in the history of NASCAR racing
- Son of Eddie Wood, who took over the day-to-day of Wood Brothers Racing in the 1980s with his brother, Jon's uncle, Len
- Began racing go-karts at the age of twelve, and won sixteen races in two years
- Won twenty-seven victories in the Champ Kart Division
- 1996 World Karting Association North Carolina dirt champion
- 1997 WKA North Carolina asphalt champion
- 1998 Rookie of the Year in Allison Legacy cars
- 1999 Rookie of the Year at New River Valley Speedway
- Raced in the Hooters Pro Cup Series in 2000
- Won first NASCAR Craftsman Truck Series race in 2003
- In 2005 started first full NASCAR Busch Series as the driver of the family-owned Wood Brothers Ford

On the Move

If the NASCAR Nextel Cup Series does not give you enough to choose from, or if you just have not quite found your guy yet, fear not. The Craftsman Truck and Busch Series have lots of HBITs (Hot Boys In Training) that are just about race-ready.

These young guns are in the process of working their way up to the Big Pa Pa of stock car racing, the NASCAR Nextel Cup Series. Oh, let me count the ways of why one might consider catching an HBIT . . .

The HBIT List

Aaron Fike—Truck Series

Chad McCumbee—Truck Series

Erik Darnell—Truck Series

Justin Diercks—2005 NASCAR AutoZone Elite Midwest Series champion

David Ragan—Busch Series

Steven Wallace—Truck Series

Regan Smith—Busch Series

Todd Kluever—Busch Series

Mark McFarland—Busch Series

Timothy Peters—Busch Series

Johnny Sauter—Busch Series

Auggie Vidovich—NASCAR Toyota All-Star Showdown winner

Brandon Whitt—Truck Series

Girlfriend to Girlfriend

The Busch Series drivers feel the Cup boys have an unfair advantage when racing in the Busch Series events due to the experience they bring from the Cup side of things, which could not be any closer to the truth.

How They Met

PATTIE AND KYLE PETTY

She was a Miss Winston, attending graduate school at Appalachian State University; he was still in high school, a budding race car driver looking for his first ride. Pattie and Kyle had all the makings of a great romance that would stand the test of time.

It all started when Pattie (who was working for RJ Reynolds Tobacco Company at the time) was scheduled to be Miss Winston for the 1976 weekend racing events at the famous Fairgrounds Speedway in Nashville, Tennessee. Kyle was at the track watching his father, the legendary Richard Petty, race. The two hooked up when Pattie took note that Kyle was limping around with a broken leg. She felt sorry for him and decided to strike up a conversation. It did not take long for the two to feel the chemistry between them. They both lived in the same area back home in North Carolina and they both had a love for horses.

Pattie was a little concerned about their age difference—so she decided to keep their budding relationship secret until she could figure out where things were going. She was so concerned, in fact, that she always had another friend with her when she and Kyle would meet up.

It was soon after Kyle graduated from high school that he made it clear how he felt about his relationship with Pattie. In July of 1978, while the two were feeding yearlings, Kyle proposed. Pattie quickly set her wedding plans into motion, but not until she took care of one piece of business. It was a rule that Miss Winstons were not allowed to date drivers. Pattie called her bosses at Winston to let them know she would have to resign due to the fact that she was about to become Mrs. Kyle Petty.

Kyle and Pattie were married on February 4, 1979, at Kepley's Barn, a local BBQ place in town, surrounded by the people that meant the most to them. It was only a week later when Kyle competed in his very first race, an ARCA event at Daytona that he surprised everyone by winning.

The Top Five Reasons to Snatch Him on the Way Up

1. The NASCAR Nextel Cup mentality has not taken hold yet.
2. Less competition for his affection—fewer girls throw themselves at the guys running in the Truck and Busch Series.
3. He is still trainable.
4. The Truck Series has a much shorter schedule, at twenty-five events a year versus the thirty-six-race schedule offered up by the Cup Series and the thirty-five-race schedule in the Busch Series. Less time racing equals more time with you.
5. The Truck and Busch Series drivers are much more relaxed than the Cup Series drivers. While the two series are popular in their own right, neither receives as much attention, and therefore there is less demand for drivers' time, leading to more relaxed drivers.

The Top Five . . .

PLACES YOU WILL *NOT* SPOT A SINGLE NASCAR DRIVER

1. Chuck E Cheese's
2. Sephora
3. Hair salon
4. Commercial airline (Hello, they have their own planes!)
5. PTA meeting

Match the Driver

How well do you know your driver? Take your best shot to see if you know him as well as you thought.

A. Kasey Kahne	1. Owns Eldora Speedway
B. Carl Edwards	2. Uncle won the Indianapolis 500 four times
C. Tony Stewart	3. Licensed helicopter pilot
D. Greg Biffle	4. Best friends with Rusty Wallace
E. Robby Gordon	5. Brother Kayle works on his crew
F. Jon Wood	6. Owns a dog named Killer
G. Casey Mears	7. Family has owned Cup Series teams since 1950
H. Jamie McMurray	8. Worked as a substitute teacher
I. Dale Earnhardt Jr.	9. Made an appearance in a Burger King commercial

Answer Key: A-5, B-8, C-1, D-3, E-9, F-7, G-2, H-4, I-6

Pit Road Wisdom

We all have a vision of who we think our *Mr. Right* is, but sometimes he is not exactly who you thought he was, or, more importantly, the one who is right for you. Because each person is unique, it is important that you get to know someone for the person that he is, and not judge him only by what he looks like or seems to be on the surface.

Part Two

⚙

The Green Flag

"Go, baby, go!"

How to Walk the Walk and Talk the Talk

Now that you have the basics and know your driver, let's get down to the good stuff . . . how to grab your guy's attention.

There are many ways a girl can catch the eye of her favorite guy, but what I have always found to be the best-case scenario is one that looks like it was a chance meeting. You know, one that was not planned twelve months—or even twelve days—in advance. A few examples:

- Bumping into Carl Edwards at the supermarket in Talladega during a race weekend is a *chance meeting*.
  Staking out the frozen food section in Columbia, Missouri, when you live in Nashville, Tennessee, *is not*.
- Being introduced to Jamie McMurray at a charity event to raise money for autism is a *chance meeting*. Showing up on his doorstep to challenge him for a radio-controlled car race in his backyard *is not*.
- Saying hello to David Stremme during a pit tour at Lowe's Motor Speedway is a *chance meeting*. Stepping in front of his mountain bike when he's on a camping trip with his buddies *is not*.

So how is a girl to meet a guy who spends most of his time driving at 180 mph? Confucius say . . . *in order to*

The Top Five . . .
MEETING SCENARIOS

1. You are his waitress at his favorite restaurant.
2. You run into him in the pet food aisle in the grocery store.
3. You just so happen to have car problems at the entrance to his neighborhood.
4. You cut his mom's hair.
5. Your best friend is his PR rep.

catch a tiger by the tail, you have to run fast and grab hold. Well, maybe not exactly, but catching a tiger by the tail might be easier than slowing down a driver. Chins up, girls . . . we have some work to do.

The older I get, the wiser my mom becomes. Remember the "first impressions are everything" advice our mothers planted in our heads from the time we were born? The first impression you leave on your driver is your direct link to his memory bank. You want to catch his eye, grab his attention, and leave him wondering who you are.

The Walk

Let's start with your walk—how you carry yourself. What does your walk say about you? Do you mean business, are you a party girl, or are you content staying at home watching a movie?

There are four main types of walks: *Superspeedway, Road Course, Short Track,* and *Intermediate.* Let's figure out which one is yours, and what it tells a driver about you.

Superspeedway—A bold (heavy-footed) and abrupt walk with attitude
- High-maintenance
- Likes to party
- Easily angered
- Noncommittal, plays the field
- Self-assured
- Likes to talk

Road Course—A smooth waltz-type walk, a gentle glide to the left and right
- Hard to read, others do not know where you stand
- Likes to party but enjoys staying at home at times
- A bit wishy-washy
- Flip-flops between favorite drivers, one this week, another next week
- The life of the party
- Always ready for a new challenge

The Top Five . . .

WAYS TO PRACTICE, PRACTICE, PRACTICE

1. Check your walk (for the 100th) time in front of a mirror.
2. Recite your "first hello" to your dog.
3. Make eye contact with your pet goldfish.
4. Memorize the NASCAR dictionary so you can understand his language.
5. Go shopping (again) for just the right outfit.

Short Track—Small and choppy steps, fast-paced walk
- Loyal
- Short temper
- More comfortable at home than out partying
- Argumentative
- Reclusive
- Competitive

Intermediate—A comfortable-paced, medium-step walk
- Well-balanced
- Goes with the flow
- Kind-natured
- Self-assured—almost too much at times
- Friendly
- Can either stay at home or party hearty

The Top Five . . .
GREATEST PICKUP LINES

1. You look race-ready to me.
2. Wanna bump-draft?
3. Hey baby, you are hitting all your marks.
4. Wanna get in the groove?
5. I'd trade paint with you any day.

The Talk

Just as your walk tells something about your personality, so does your talk. Have you ever caught yourself mesmerized by someone before they said a word, and then they opened their mouth and you're like . . . *ugh*?

First impressions most times are based on what you look like or how you present yourself, but the lasting impression often comes not from what you look like but from what you said.

Are you articulate, witty, self-absorbed, cocky, or just plain boring? Let's face it; sometimes we need to look in the mirror and take an inventory of who we are and what we represent. Sometimes a little *pit stop* is needed for some quick servicing . . . maybe a little *adjustment* or even a *splash of gas*.

There are four different types of talks . . . *Tight, Loose, Pushy,* and *Dialed-in.* What impression are you sending out with your talk?

Tight—A soft, tight-lipped approach that is often misread. Every word spoken is overanalyzed due to the shy and quiet demeanor of the talker.

- Shy
- Uppity
- Quiet
- Well-versed

Loose—What's on the mind is what comes out of the mouth. This is not the think-first-then-speak type of girl. Can be viewed as a motor mouth.

- Highly entertaining
- Trash talker
- Talks too much
- Confident

Girlfriend to Girlfriend

Okay, girls, the quickest way to run off your favorite heartthrob is to ask for an autograph. Trust me on this . . . think cool, calm, and collected! Now, if he asks you for yours . . . things are looking good!

Pushy—Always speaks what's on her mind. Goes after what she wants. Can be used-car-salesman-like in her approach.

- Opinionated
- Pushes oneself on others, at times too much
- Loud
- Determined

Dialed-in—Always knows exactly what to say and when to say it. Very in tune with others.

- Comfortable
- Mild-mannered
- Sincere
- Articulate

The Clothes Hanger

Why is it that no matter the situation, we girls just can't figure out what to wear?

When planning your outfit for your first meeting with your NASCAR hottie, the biggest factor is setting. Always think . . . *dress the part.* If you are at a cocktail reception, you wear a cocktail dress. If you are at a racetrack, you wear something more suitable for a day at the races. In most cases in life it is better to be overdressed than underdressed, but at a racetrack it's usually the reverse. There is no better way to stand out like a sore thumb at a track than to show up in an elegant little black number with heels and pearls, even if you do look fabulous in it. Talk about throwing the red flag!

I will get more into where to meet your favorite driver later, but for now here are my suggestions for what to wear for your first "chance meeting."

Racetrack

All right, girls, this is NOT the place to show off your new pair of stilettos or your cute little Daisy Duke shorts. Remember, there is a time and place for everything, not to mention, NASCAR is very specific about what you can wear depending on where you are at the track. If you are visiting the garage area or pit road, NASCAR has a little list of what you can and cannot do.

What to Wear

- Casual long pants or nice jeans (leave the holey ones at home)
- Nice short-sleeve shirt that covers the stomach area
- Understated jewelry—remember, standing out is not always a good thing!
- Comfortable walking shoes (must be closed-toe)

What NOT to Wear

- Open-toe shoes—this includes cute little sandals and flip-flops
- Shorts or skirts
- Tank tops—all shirts must cover the shoulder

Track Function (Outside Garage Area and Pit Road)

This certainly allows you the opportunity to let loose just a bit, as NASCAR has no rules outside the secured areas. Don't forget to consider the weather—you will want to be comfortable, and not overdressed. Think casual with an attitude.

What to Wear

- Nice shorts (not too short)
- Simple tank top or casual shirt
- Casual pants or nice jeans
- Shorter-length skirt (a few inches above the knee)
- Comfortable (but cute) walking shoes
- Simple, understated jewelry

Girlfriend to Girlfriend

There is nothing worse than seeing a girl at the track wearing gobs of jewelry or jewelry not appropriate for her attire. Picture this—nice jeans, a cute shirt, a great pair of stylish tennis shoes, *and* three-tier chandelier earrings with matching three-tier necklace, bracelet, and ring. I don't think so! Trust me when I say, save the jewels for another day.

Girlfriend to Girlfriend

As much as I love my cute little flip-flops (I have them in every color), most guys think they are a bit trashy. Tread lightly when feeling the need for a night out on the town with flip-flops in tow.

Autograph Signings

Girls, this is what you have been waiting for, but don't get too crazy. Always think you want to be noticed for the right reasons.

What to Wear

- Cute short skirt and tank set
- Holey jeans with understated top
- Nice shorts with simple top
- Jewelry to your liking—*No overkill please!*
- Sandals or cute pumps (a must)

Media Events/Sponsor Cocktail Parties

Those chandelier earrings you have been dying to bring out can now make their debut. You can officially strut your stuff in high fashion. If you have it . . . *flaunt it!*

Did You Know. . .

The last hour of practice before the start of each single event is called Happy Hour.

fast fact

Nascar Nextel Cup Series teams spend an enormous amount of time each year preparing for the races. Each NASCAR Nextel Cup Series event allows a certain amount of time on the track for the drivers to practice their car setups and to check their track time against other drivers. This is basically free time for the drivers to hone their skills on each track. After all, practice means they'll be perfect—or at least as close to perfect as they can get.

What to Wear

- Dinner suit
- Cocktail dress
- Floor-length gown
- Jewelry to your taste and style (high fashion or simple understated)

Where to Find NASCAR Hunks

So, how in the world can a gal even catch up to a guy who's always racing at 180 mph, much less meet him? Believe it or not, it's easier than you think. The rule of thumb with racers is you have to go where the action is. If there isn't racing . . . there probably aren't any race car drivers either. The best place to find out where a driver will be, from autograph sessions to charity events, is their Web site (for Web site addresses check out "The Starting Lineup" in Part One). Many tracks also offer special autograph sessions on race weekends. Always check the Web site of the track you are attending before you get there to plan accordingly.

Race Track

This is the obvious place to track a driver down. The NASCAR Nextel Cup Series schedule makes it so that the drivers have to arrive at the track either on Thursday night of race week or early Friday morning. The majority of the drivers have private motor coaches waiting for them at the track when they arrive. The race schedule for most tracks places the Cup Series event on Sunday, although some races are on Saturday night.

The drivers spend the majority of their time at the

Girlfriend to Girlfriend

I met Davey at Summerville Speedway right outside Charleston, South Carolina, when I was only twenty-two years old, sitting on the bed of a pickup truck minding my own business. My initial meeting with Davey was all of ten minutes, and I probably only said five words to him before he darted out of town like a thief in the night.

The Top Five . . .

WAYS TO GET A GARAGE PASS

1. Buy a special package—some tracks offer special ticket packages that include a garage pass.
2. Use a race team connection (e.g., your second cousin's high school buddy works in the pit crew).
3. Act like you are a driver's long-lost cousin.
4. Use a sponsor connection (e.g., your best friend's uncle is a VP at Nextel).
5. Grab hold of a rolling pit box and hope you are not spotted.

track either in their race car or in the garage area with their team. A garage pass will give you the best access to where the action is. But a garage pass is not an easy get because of the nature of the area—secured, dangerous, and busy. NASCAR allows each team, car owner, and sponsor a certain number of garage passes for each event. Most tracks that offer the garage pass special will only allow you to tour the garage area with a group and a tour guide. This is more of a "rush 'em through" approach to visiting the driver's workplace.

Autograph Sessions

Outside of the race track, this is the easiest place to put your best foot forward with your favorite guy. Since NASCAR Nextel Cup Series drivers have quite a bit of sponsor money, that means they have many commitments to those sponsors. One of the most valuable tools for a sponsor is the time commitment of the driver, which is all laid out in the driver-sponsor contract.

Most of the drivers make anywhere from six to twenty appearances a year for their sponsors. Many of those appearances are autograph sessions that are open to the public. Sponsors like to put their drivers out there to pull people into their stores and businesses, or to attract them to their products.

fast fact

A pit box is a traveling (on wheels) cabinet used in the garage area as well as pit road. It contains all the tools the pit crew may need for race day activities—pit stops, car adjustments, and so forth. The box also houses the computerized equipment the team uses during the race to determine track speeds, tire wear, and gas mileage. Many wives and girlfriends choose to sit on top of the pit box during the race. This gives them a better view of the pit stall and race track.

The majority of the drivers actually enjoy getting out and meeting their fans. Autograph sessions are a perfect opportunity for you—the drivers are normally more relaxed and laid-back at these functions than at the stressful racetrack.

Sponsor Functions

Again, the drivers are tied in to many sponsor functions as a part of their sponsor-driver relationship. Many times drivers will appear at a sponsor dinner or event in the host city during a race weekend, or even during the weeknights between race weekends.

Charity Events

Just about every driver is personally involved in a charity. Most charity events are open to the public due largely to the money they may donate to the charity.

Restaurants

Drivers do not eat out on the road like they used to. Most of the drivers eat at their motor coach in the drivers' compound, as most of their coach drivers also serve as the cook, or at least make arrangements to have food for the driver. But don't lose heart—they still visit local restaurants on occasion, even while on the road traveling the NASCAR Nextel Cup Series schedule. Keep in mind the track schedule before heading out for dinner in hopes of meeting your guy face-to-face. It will usually be at least two hours after the end of practice that drivers make their way to a restaurant.

Most of the teams and drivers live near Charlotte, North Carolina, which makes restaurants in the Mooresville, Concord, Harrisburg, Lake Norman, and Charlotte areas most promising for driver sightings. You are more likely to spot a driver out on the town Monday through Wednesday since the drivers (under most circumstances) are not home Thursday through Sunday.

How They Met

BOBBY AND JUDY ALLISON

Bobby and Judy Allison have the classic he-said, she-said story of how they met. Bobby believes they met when Judy was only thirteen years old at the race shop of Ralph Stark, who was married to Judy's sister, Carolyn. Judy, however, believes this was just a figment of Bobby's imagination and that they really met for the first time when she was sixteen years old and a spectator at the Hollywood Speedway in Hollywood, Florida, where Bobby just happened to be racing that night. It was after the race that Judy and Bobby had their first encounter . . . so she says.

Judy was at a local eatery that was popular with the racers later that night when Bobby walked in with a date on his arm. He sat directly across from Judy so that he could not only see her but make sure she could see him, even though he had a date tucked in tight beside him. They went their separate ways that night, but not for long.

A few nights later, a mysterious knock on the door of her sister's home turned out to be the twist of fate that would totally change Judy's life around. When Judy opened the door, there stood a slicked-up Bobby Allison. He said he was there to see Ralph Stark to talk about a car part, but she knew that was about the furthest thing from the truth. After a brief conversation, Bobby asked her to ride with him to the race shop, and she reluctantly agreed. When they arrived, the shop was closed. Judy's initial reaction to Bobby was not a good one. In fact, she decided she didn't want to see him again.

Several weeks passed before the two crossed paths again. This time the sparks flew on and off the track. Bobby was racing at West Palm Beach Speedway, but crashed out of the race early. He spotted Judy in the grandstands and decided to join her to watch the rest of the racing. That was the night Bobby and Judy agreed there was something more to them than what they initially thought. The only problem was the next morning she was moving with her mother to Orlando, 200 miles away. Bobby, being the trouper that he was, drove the 400-mile round-trip to Orlando to see Judy every other week for over a year.

The next year (1960) Bobby and Judy were married and moved to a little house in Oakland Park, Florida. It was soon after that Judy quit her job and started traveling the racing circuit with Bobby. After Davey and Bonnie, the first of their four children, were born, Bobby and Judy packed up and moved to Hueytown, Alabama, to be closer to the eye of the racing storm.

Bobby enjoyed racing until an accident in 1988 at Pocono Raceway ended his illustrious career. Despite their hardships, somehow they have kept their love for one another and their love of racing alive. Bobby and Judy still travel to a handful of races each year and remain two of the strongest ambassadors for the sport.

Nightclubs/Hot Spots

What do good-looking, successful, young, single guys do to wind down when they're not on the track? You got it, spend a night out on the town! Dale Earnhardt Jr. and his posse have given new meaning to Party All Night. Tony Stewart and many other hard-charging drivers have said keeping up with Jr. is a tough row to hoe.

NASCAR Nextel Cup Series drivers are no different from many other unattached adults—they love to find the hot spots and party down. You can often find a driver or two out at hotel and restaurant bars, nightclubs, and even dance clubs in racing cities as the circuit travels the country. The most frequented party spots are in Charlotte, since most drivers live in the area. The most common night to see drivers out is Wednesday as it is not only midweek, but also the night before most teams head out for the next race.

The Top Five . . .
DRIVER-FAVORITE CHARLOTTE-AREA HOT SPOTS

1. Vinnie's (Exit 33 off I-77)
2. The Wine Room of Afton Village (Exit 54 off I-85)
3. Bar Charlotte (Uptown Charlotte)
4. 10 O'Clock Charlie's (Highway 150 in Mooresville)
5. Rusty Rudder (Exit 28 off I-77)

Test Sessions

The NASCAR Nextel Cup Series teams have a certain number of tests each year. The teams travel to a particular track to test for one or two days. Some teams even go to non–NASCAR Nextel Cup Series tracks to test. These test sessions are very low-key and draw very few on-lookers. Some test sessions are private—no one can watch the drivers on the track—but others not only allow observers, but also have a time allotted for au-tographs and meet-and-greets. The non–Cup Series tracks like Nashville and Kentucky are very popular test tracks for the drivers mainly because these are not regulated by NASCAR. The teams can test at these tracks as many times as they like without stepping out-side the allotted NASCAR tests. These tracks are very fan-friendly and most always allow spectators to attend the test sessions.

The Top Five . . .

TEST TRACKS FOR MEET-AND-GREETS

1. Daytona
2. Lowe's (Charlotte)
3. Indianapolis
4. Nashville—non–Cup Series track
5. Kentucky Speedway—non–Cup Series track

Short Track/Dirt Track Racing

If racers aren't racing, they are thinking about racing. Most of the drivers you see in the NASCAR Nextel Cup Series would race anything with wheels, anytime. Many different tracks around the country grab the attention of Cup Series drivers for off-weekend and weeknight races. These racing situations are very low-key, but with high energy and smaller crowds, which make them a great place to meet a driver.

Hometown

The majority of drivers live in the Charlotte area, but all drivers have a place to call home. Many of the drivers' moms now live in the Charlotte vicinity, but some still live in their hometowns. No matter how far a driver goes in his career, few forget where they came from, and home calls them back several times a year. (Check out "The Starting Lineup" in Part One to find out your favorite driver's hometown.)

Gyms

Many of the drivers find great relief in working out and go to great measures to scope out gyms in race cities. Gyms in the Lake Norman area are the most popular for drivers as most live in the vicinity. Many drivers have gym memberships (such as to the YMCA) that enable them to use facilities in other race cities.

Girlfriend to Girlfriend

The Harris Teeter in Lake Norman (between Exits 33 and 36 of I-77) is where many drivers do their grocery shopping. Most of the drivers live in the vicinity, making this grocery store a haven for race car drivers.

Grocery Store

Okay, yes, the majority of race car drivers do their own grocery shopping, believe it or not. The area a driver lives in determines which grocery he uses. Since a greater number of the drivers live in the Lake Norman area, it is safe to say that most shop for groceries in that area. Keep in mind, you won't find them shopping for frozen pizza on a race weekend. Best times to catch them are Sunday nights through Wednesday evenings.

Chiropractor's Office

A little bump here, a little bump there . . . maybe a crash or two in between. A day at the office for a race car driver makes for a chiropractor's dream. Many NASCAR drivers have standing Monday morning appointments with their friendly chiropractor.

fast fact

The driver and his team ultimately decide whether their non-Cup test sessions will be private or open to the public. It is not uncommon for big-name drivers like Dale Earnhardt Jr. and Jeff Gordon to hold private tests.

Coffee Shop

A little java can get anybody's motor running and NASCAR drivers are no exception. The only thing we are missing is a Starbucks-sponsored car!

PLACES TO CATCH A DRIVER IN HIS HOMETOWN

1. Momma's church
2. Schools the driver attended
3. Momma's favorite restaurant
4. Local hospital—visiting patients
5. Christmas Parade/Key to the City ceremony—Most all drivers receive invitations to command the Christmas Parade or receive a Key to the City

The Meet-and-Greet

Okay, girls, this is where the rubber meets the road ∴ that one and only, very first meeting of the minds. When I met Davey at Summerville Speedway in 1988, I was rumbling on the inside as I somehow knew he was special, but I stayed calm, cool, and unaffected. He would admit later that my nonchalant attitude was one of the things that caught his attention. Here are a few things to keep in mind when meeting Mr. Handsome for the very first time:

Tips for the Meet-and-Greet

- **Keep your cool**—You do not want to seem over-zealous, overeager, or too excited . . . remember the three Cs: cool, calm, and collected!
- **Appear to be unaffected by his stardom**—I know this is a tough one, but guys are so turned off by girls who are into them just because they drive race cars. Drivers want to know you like them for who they are, not for what they do.
- **Make eye contact**—Don't stare, but do make that one-on-one eye contact that makes him see into you.
- **Speak less/listen more**—Okay, girls, many of us get real chatty when we are a bit nervous. Take a breath through your nose, and speak slowly and softly.
- **Do not be too provocative**—In most cases guys like girls who can ulti-

Girlfriend to Girlfriend

When Davey asked for my number when we first met, I gave him my work number. It was not until after he called me at least five times at work that I decided to give him my home number.

mately be taken home to Momma. A little sassiness is okay, but be careful not to overdo it with the sexiness factor.

- **Let him ask for your number**—Never ask for his.
- **Do not gush about the race, drivers, or NASCAR**—Keep it real.
- **Never wear racing paraphernalia**—Not a NASCAR T-shirt, hat, pin . . . zilch . . . nothing! You do not want to look like a groupie!

The Top Five . . .

SHORT TRACKS TO MEET YOUR FAVORITE DRIVER

1. Greenville Pickens Speedway (Greenville, South Carolina)
2. Hickory Motor Speedway (Hickory, North Carolina)
3. Talladega Dirt Track (Talladega, Alabama)
4. Lowe's Dirt Track (Charlotte, North Carolina)
5. Eldora Speedway (Rossburg, Ohio)

The First Date

Meeting your driver is the easy part; getting that important first date is a little trickier. Any driver can attempt to qualify for a race, but it's the drivers that stand above the rest that make the field. Once he figures out that you stand above the competition, he will be racing to ask you out.

Where He Might Take You

- **His next race**—Now, that's what I call a first date!
- **Short track**—This is actually a lot of fun, to go with your guy to a local short track and watch (probably one of his buddies). You'll see racing at its best. Remember . . . racers love racing and can't seem to get enough of it!
- **Charity event**—This can be tons of fun if he is not on all night. There is nothing worse than going somewhere with him when he is serving as a celebrity guest and he takes off to do his duties and leaves you standing there wishing you weren't missing *Grey's Anatomy*.
- **Dinner and a movie**—This is the classic (no-fail) first date. Confucius say . . . *always check teeth after dinner or one might not get date number two.*
- **Romantic dinner for two at his place**—*Ooh la la* . . . now we're talking. A little dinner by candlelight can rev up anyone's engine.
- **A day on his boat**—This is fun with a capital F. There is nothing better than basking in the sun with your favorite guy with no engines revving

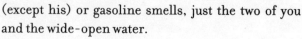

(except his) or gasoline smells, just the two of you and the wide-open water.

- **Chips, salsa, and a Margarita (or two)**—Race car drivers love Mexican food. Don't be surprised if your first date consists of tamales and refried beans. Confucius say . . . *eat beans make you pass gas.* Liz say, may want to bring along some Beano.
  - **Clubbing**—This can be really good or really bad, but interesting either way. Let's hope he knows how to dance as well as he drives a race car.
    - **Team cookout**—This is a great way for you to see him with his team away from the track. As long as he does not leave you stranded, this can be a very fun time. *Bonus*—if he is asking you to accompany him to a team event on the first date, you are probably assured other dates to come.
- **NASCAR Nextel Cup Series Awards Banquet**—Your chances of having your first date consist of a private plane to New York, accommodations at the Waldorf, and being seen on national television with him are pretty slim—but dreaming never hurt anyone!

Good (and Not So Good) Topics of Conversation

As with any setting (a first date or job interview) there are always the right things to say and the wrong things to say. Staying true to yourself is the key, but always keep in mind that what one thinks is sometimes best left unsaid.

The Good—These topics all show a personal interest in him and what makes him tick without being too intrusive:

- His career goals
- His family
- His (outside-of-racing) interests
- His home
- Cars!!

The Bad—These topics are better left for date four, five, or six (or later). You might want to have a little foundation to stand firmly on before opening these cans of worms:

- Politics
- Religion
- His salary and benefits package
- Family issues
- Racing rumors

The Ugly—There is no better way to guarantee a second date *never* coming than by bringing up one of these subjects. These are the definite "think it but don't say it" topics of conversation:
- Why his house is not as big as Jeff Gordon's
- Why he never runs in the top ten on race day
- His thoughts on his never winning a championship
- Who that girl you saw walking him to his car on race day on TV last weekend was
- His thoughts on him being the marrying kind

How They Met
DONNA AND BOBBY LABONTE

While some may say love at first sight does not exist, Donna Labonte believes it to be true. She was still in high school, working at a Revco Pharmacy in Thomasville, North Carolina, when a handsome stranger walked in. She knew the minute they made eye contact that he was the one.

Bobby Labonte was working in the race shop of his older brother, Terry, who was a driver on the NASCAR Nextel Cup Series circuit. The shop was conveniently located close to where Donna worked, so Bobby would often pop into the store, but being the shy guy that he is, never had much to say. It was not until one night right before closing that Donna got the message loud and clear that Bobby was interested in her.

Bobby came into the store to talk to Donna briefly and then abruptly left just before the store closed. When Donna reached her car, there was a note from Bobby with his phone number on it. Donna made the first call, which led to (less than twenty-four hours later) their first date, at the Pizza Inn.

Donna went on to attend college after she graduated from high school in 1984. Bobby's life was already wrapped tight around the racing world as his own driving career was getting into high gear.

Donna graduated from Guilford Technical Community College in 1986 and went to work for a neurosurgeon. The two continued to date while Bobby was chasing his dreams all over the country. When Bobby made the jump to the NASCAR Busch Series, he decided he wanted Donna by his side . . . as his wife. After eight years of dating, Bobby popped the question in October 1990. The two were married the following Easter weekend.

Girlfriend to Girlfriend

Always let him lead the way with the good-night kiss. Race car drivers are no different from most guys in that they like to be the initiator. If he is thinking a simple peck and you are thinking you will display your best French . . . things might get a little sloppy . . . literally!

Ways to Guarantee Date Number Two

- Downplay his racing efforts and display a sincere interest in him
- Leave your résumé for your next job interview
- Show your softer side, as in personal interests and philanthropy efforts
- Let him call the shots—at least for the first date
- Save your super-sexy revealing clothes for after you win his heart

Pit Road Wisdom

As with most things in life, there is more than one way to do just about anything. I have found with life's twists and turns (and in NASCAR racing there are lots) a good sense of humor will take you far. Whether it's your favorite NASCAR driver or the boy next door (if you're lucky, they are one and the same), staying true to yourself is what will separate you from everyone else.

Part Three

The Yellow

Flag

Caution! Danger up ahead!

The Boyfriend Quiz

So, just what makes a good candidate for a boyfriend . . . easy on the eyes, driven, exciting, and successful? NASCAR drivers come in lots of different shapes and sizes but what are *you* looking for in a driver? Does *he* pass *your* test?

1. If you love blond-haired guys you might want to check out:
Jamie McMurray, Carl Edwards, Jon Wood, Clint Bowyer, Brian Vickers, Dale Earnhardt Jr.

2. If age is important, you might want to see who fits the bill for you:
18–22—Kyle Busch, Reed Sorenson
23–27—Denny Hamlin, Kasey Kahne, Paul Menard, Martin Truex Jr., Brian Vickers, Jon Wood
28–32—Clint Bowyer, Dale Earnhardt Jr., Carl Edwards, Jamie McMurray, Casey Mears, Elliott Sadler, David Stremme
33–37—Greg Biffle, Tony Stewart, Robby Gordon
38 and up—Sorry, girls, these guys are taken

3. If loving animals is a must for you, check out:
Greg Biffle, Elliott Sadler, Dale Earnhardt Jr., Casey Mears

4. If wearing heels on a date is a must, check out which driver is tall enough to make the cut:

5'11" and up—Clint Bowyer, Kyle Busch, Dale Earnhardt Jr., Carl Edwards, Denny Hamlin, Elliott Sadler, David Stremme, Martin Truex Jr., Brian Vickers

5. Do you love guys who drive fast?
Yes—Take your pick
No—You might have to try another profession

6. If the perfect date for you with your favorite driver is going to a short track on an off–NEXTEL Cup weekend, you might want to take a second look at:
Tony Stewart, Kasey Kahne, Dale Earnhardt Jr.

7. If you believe that real men drive Chevys, check out:
Tony Stewart, Dale Earnhardt Jr., Denny Hamlin, Casey Mears, Martin Truex Jr., Kyle Busch, Paul Menard, Clint Bowyer

8. If you would rather be on the golf course, you might like to invite:
Elliott Sadler, Jon Wood, Brian Vickers

9. If working out is your thing, check out these abs:
Carl Edwards, Reed Sorenson

10. If you love to mountain-bike, you may want to hang out with:
Carl Edwards, Robby Gordon, David Stremme

11. If living on the water is a must for you, check out:
Casey Mears, Carl Edwards, Dale Earnhardt Jr., Clint Bowyer, Tony Stewart

12. If you love playing video games, you may hit it off with:
Dale Earnhardt Jr., Kyle Busch, Martin Truex Jr., Denny Hamlin, Reed Sorenson, Brian Vickers

13. If you love winter sports, bundle up and join one of these guys in the snow:
Kasey Kahne, Casey Mears, Paul Menard, David Stremme, Martin Truex Jr.

Things Every Girl Should Know About Racers

Race car drivers are a rare breed, and the fast-paced life of a driver's wife is not as easy or as glamorous as it looks. Drivers' wives in many cases give up their own dreams in order to chase their guys around every race track from Charlotte to California, and many states in between. There really ought to be a cup for drivers' wives as well, they all deserve one!

Before you set your sights (and heart) on a long-term relationship with your favorite driver, there a few things you must know. Some of these insights may even surprise you.

Twelve Things to Know Before Dating a NASCAR Driver

1. **They rarely sit still.** Now that might not seem like much to you, but trust me, the high-paced energy of a race car driver can grow old at times. Drivers are so used to going *full speed ahead* that in many cases they have a hard time kicking back and letting go.
2. **It is racing 24/7.** Their brains are turning left even when the cars aren't. If racers aren't racing, they are thinking about what they need to do to their car next—how to get more speed, how to hit that magic setup, what track is next, and so on.
3. **The phone always rings.** If it is not the car owner, it's the crew chief or maybe the PR rep who needs the driver to make just one more call. As with any big business, there is always something that needs to be discussed.

4. **Vacations are few and far between.** That is, unless you call Darlington Raceway a great vacation spot. Due to the long race season, most guys just want to stay home when the schedule allows a weekend off.

5. **The NASCAR schedule.** Whew, it is rough at best. You better make sure you like racing too, or you will not be a happy camper for ten months out of the year. NASCAR Nextel Cup Series racing kicks off in February and does not wrap up until mid-November, not to mention the Awards Banquet the first weekend of December. It is a long and grueling schedule, which wreaks havoc on long-distance relationships and any downtime.

6. **Losing is tough.** These guys are fiercely competitive, which means when Lady Luck does not shine brightly on them, their disappointment is hard to hide. Some guys are prone to anger or temper tantrums when things don't go their way, while others just prefer not to talk at all. This can be tough on women who want to fix things and make everything okay—and trust me, girls, it isn't something you can fix.

7. **Accidents, sadly, do happen.** NASCAR Nextel Cup Series racing is dangerous, there is no way around it. Some girls handle their stress differently from others. This is a part of the deal you better take note of in the very beginning. You either learn to cope or you sit it out. Drivers have very little understanding and compassion for the shaky nerves of their significant others. In their eyes, it's just the way it is.

8. **They don't talk about their fear.** And neither should you. Fear is a four-letter word not used by NASCAR drivers. What "could happen" is handled by the safety equipment they wear. In other words, the fact that they wear safety equipment means that they respect danger but do not give in to fear. You could easily call it racer's denial.

9. **There is little family time.** These guys are on the road more than they are at home. That leaves a very small amount of time for their families, which is why the married drivers take their wives and kids with them on the road. Parents, siblings, and good friends of the drivers sometimes come out on the road so they can see their loved one. If not, they would most likely not see them at all.

10. **Flying is a part of life.** If you have a fear of flying this is not the life for you. Drivers fly almost every weekend on the NASCAR Nextel Cup circuit. The majority of drivers own their own planes, but some fly on their car owner's plane or buddy up with another driver. It is usually not until

a driver's second or third year on the circuit that he purchases his own airplane, unless he has had early success.

11. **Drivers never forget a race.** They have an uncanny way of remembering every race they have ever been in, from where they ran to who got in their way to what the weather conditions were. Sorry, this doesn't mean they will never forget a birthday or anniversary. A little selective memory banking perhaps.

12. **Many drivers are superstitious.** Who would have thought? Peanuts, the color green, and fifty-dollar bills are all things drivers stay clear of at the racetrack. Few drivers can tell you why they are superstitious or why to dodge the color green. The fact is, they steer clear because they have always heard it through the racing grapevine. Kind of like an old fishing story . . . the longer it goes on the bigger the fish gets.

Did You Know. . .

The majority of racers have their own motor coaches and take them to almost all the Cup Series events.

The Top Five . . .

THINGS MOMMA NEVER TOLD ME ABOUT RACE CAR DRIVERS

1. They talk to their crew chief in their sleep.
2. They will not let anyone else drive, nor will they ask for directions.
3. They eat lots of takeout.
4. They practice thanking their sponsors every morning in front of the mirror.
5. They think finishing second means being the first loser.

Pit Stop Strategy

There are many different strategies that go into play each week in a NASCAR Nextel Cup Series race—which lap to pit on, four tires or gamble on two, stickers or scuffs. These race day strategies play an integral part in the outcome of a race.

Top Five Track Strategy Issues

1. **When and where**—Teams carefully plan when to come in for a pit stop. Pit strategy can make the difference between winning and losing a race. Pit stop strategy is all about track positioning—where you go in for a pit stop and where you come out.
2. **Fuel gambles**—Teams map out their fuel before each race. They know exactly how many laps they can go (for the most part) before needing fuel. Drivers are coached on how to conserve fuel, which could make or break a win for a driver and his team.
3. **Tires**—Do teams take two tires on a pit stop, or change all four? Do they use stickers or scuffs? These are all questions the crew chief has to answer on any given pit stop. The rule of thumb is new tires run faster, but it takes longer to get four,

which goes back to track positioning. Whoever gets out first is closer up front on the restart of the race.

4. **Race traffic**—Not all cars on the track are in race contention, which basically means racing for a win. When the lead cars are battling on the track they have to work their way through cars that are not racing for the lead. The non-race-contention cars are referred to as lapped traffic. All drivers race differently, but the ones who can ease in and out of race traffic usually end up out front.

5. **Who's your buddy?**—Having a buddy on the track is a very good thing, especially if it is Daytona or Talladega where you need drafting partners. Racing buddies can help block traffic or even open up spaces for their running partner. Two cars, in many cases, run better than one.

So, how does this apply to catching a driver? Well, just as the drivers have their strategy on the track, we gals have our own tricks off the track. Here are a few ideas to use racing maneuvers to steal your favorite driver's attention.

Strategies for Revving Up Your Chances of Meeting Your Guy

The Draft

Cars race together to achieve faster speeds. Cars running in the draft conserve fuel, reduce stress on the engines, and run faster together than a car running alone or outside of the draft.

How to apply it: A group of girls move in on a guy—safety in numbers. The idea is that several girls have a better run at the guy than one girl on her own. It should be noted that in a draft situation it must be determined who is the lead girl. It should also be noted that the lead girl may not be who the driver feels is his best draft partner, which can leave the prearranged leader *hung out to dry.*

The Bump Draft

When a car running in the draft nudges the rear bumper of the car in front. The bump is used to give the front car a little boost.

How to apply it: Two girls team up to meet their favorite driver but with the understanding that one girl will lead the way while the other runs steadily behind. Once the right time comes, the second girl will give her leader a little

The Top Five . . .

WAYS TO SHOW HIM HOW MUCH YOU CARE

1. You sleep with his helmet.
2. You shave his car number on your dog's head.
3. You name your cat after him.
4. You memorize all the car parts.
5. You tell him he ran well even when he finished forty-third.

push to move her way out front making it very clear to the driver who his draft partner should be.

The Slingshot

When a car steals the good air of the car he is attempting to pass. The driver attempting the slingshot must promptly turn his car to the right or left of the direct competitor and use the opposing car's air to pass with. This is a very complicated maneuver that few can pull off.

How to apply it: A prearranged situation provides an obnoxious (what-not-to-do-when-meeting-a-NASCAR-driver) girl and her cool, calm, and collected counterpart. The obnoxious girl will lead the way, making it clear that she is not the one. Once that point is made, the cool-headed (or so he thinks) girl steals the stage from her friend and passes her by.

Loving Me—Loving You

Have you ever heard the phrase *you have to love yourself before you can love someone else*? Take it for what it is worth but what I can tell you is this—*who you are and what you represent is what you are sharing with someone else. If you take care of yourself, not only do you feel better about yourself, but it radiates to others. Someone who does not take care of herself (or has low self-esteem) will radiate those energies. The key here is *you* first, then someone else.

All right, girls. On your feet . . . lace up those tennis shoes and let's get moving. It's time to get in your groove!

The Top Five . . .
WAYS TO LET HIM KNOW YOU ARE IN THE GROOVE

1. You can run faster than his qualifying lap.
2. You pass on dessert . . . yikes!
3. You drink more water than his pit crew during a race.
4. Your pit stop is faster than his (more on your pit stops later).
5. Thank you very much but you can change your own oil.

fast fact

The groove is where the drivers want to be on the track. Some tracks have one solid groove, while others have multiple grooves. This is where the cars run better, like driving your car on the ruts in a dirt road as opposed to on the gravel and grass.

The Body

Every integral part of your body works together to keep you running well. Are you in need of a pit stop? A little adjustment? There is no better time than now to get fired up.

Exercise

Anyone who is a NASCAR fan knows that drivers are athletes. They have to keep their bodies healthy in order to tolerate such high speeds and fast maneuvers. If you want to keep up with your guy, you'll want to be in top form. Exercise can make a world of difference not just in appearance, but in energy and how you feel.

Find something you enjoy doing, whether it's a brisk thirty-minute walk three to four times a week, a kick boxing class, or even a little tennis. Switching around workouts is a great way to keep it new, exciting, and fresh. The key is to find what makes you feel the best and what your body responds to the most. If you have trouble staying motivated, try exercising with a friend. We all need a little friendly push at times to keep the engine running. Remember, exercising is as good for the soul as it is for the body.

The Top Five . . .

WAYS TO GET YOUR BODY GROOVE ON

1. Walking
2. Step class
3. Tennis
4. Kick boxing
5. Jumping rope

Sleep

One of the most important things a driver does before a race is get a good night's sleep, and for good reason. Sleeping only four hours a night actually increases the stress level of your body. To be well rested, a person should get eight hours of sleep every night. I know what you're thinking . . . are you kidding me? I can't get eight hours every night, I have too much to do when I get home. Words of advice here—there is never enough time to do everything we think we need to do or even want to do. Scheduling a good night's sleep is one of the best appointments you can make for yourself. Pull the sheets over your head and call it a day.

Diet

It would be pretty bad for a driver not to be able to squeeze into his car for a race. Like you, most drivers have to watch what they eat. Few things in life creep up on us as quickly as the waistline. The easiest rule to remember is *food is most always healthiest in its purest form.* Foods without all the extras are what's best to feed our bodies and our minds.

The Top Five . . .
THINGS TO DO IF YOU CAN'T GET TO SLEEP

1. Dream of Kasey Kahne kissing you in Victory Lane.
2. Imagine your first walk on the beach with Dale Earnhardt Jr.
3. Picture cozying up to Carl Edwards after a long race weekend.
4. Think of skiing down the Rockies with David Stremme.
5. Put yourself in front of the fireplace with Reed Sorenson.

fast fact

The drivers and their wives are able to work out at the track, as the series has a traveling workout unit that goes to every race on the NASCAR Nextel Cup Series schedule. The unit is conveniently positioned inside the driver's motor coach compound.

Under the Hood

Did You Know...

A driver is *hung out to dry* when he gets out of the racing line or draft and quickly loses position on the track.

W hat is under the hood of a race car is as important as having wheels for the car to ride on. You can have the best-looking car on the track, but if the inner mechanics do not measure up . . . *the driver is hung out to dry.*

De-Stress

Stress is one of the most toxic things you can feed to your body. It takes more energy to stress over something than a massive power walk. Stress is believed to cause many negative effects, including but not limited to wrinkles, indigestion, heart palpitations, weight gain, and even cancer.

When you feel your stress level rising, stop to ask yourself, *will what you are stressing over matter in two months, two weeks, or even two days?* Probably not. Few things really are as life-altering as we think at the time. If you have trouble letting something go, try writing about it in your journal—you may be surprised that what you thought you were stressed about isn't the real cause. A brisk walk or talking it over with your best friend can also work wonders.

Girlfriend to Girlfriend

I can tell you that in my eighteen years in the sport many things have changed, but one thing that has stayed the same is the drivers' stand on drug use . . . it is just not accepted. Period!

Drugs and Alcohol

All right, girls, now I am not talking a glass of wine or a beer or two. I'm talking about taking drinking to the extreme. Not only is it not wise to abuse alcohol or drugs, but have you noticed that NASCAR Nextel Cup Series drivers are about the cleanest athletes out there? If you haven't, you should. NASCAR has a very strict substance abuse policy for their drivers, which leaves no room for error.

Quiet Time

Everybody needs a little downtime, but few get it. Give yourself a treat and detox your mind, body, and soul. NASCAR racing is a fast-paced lifestyle that is driven by fierce competition. The effects of that high-kicking adrenaline and jet-setting lifestyle can take their toll if one does not throw the red flag for a much needed break. Try getting a manicure, kicking back with a non-thought-provoking book (there are even some NASCAR romances out there), or give meditation or yoga a try.

When I am writing, I love to listen to soft piano music like *The Romance of Jim Brickman:* It is soothing, romantic, and mind-freeing. One of my romance writer friends actually throws on her headset and sings along to her favorite hard-charging music. Whew, to each her own!

How They Met

ARLENE AND MARK MARTIN

She was a divorced mother of four living in Batesville, Arkansas. He was a young single race car driver cutting his teeth in the American Speed Association (ASA) while living in Wisconsin. How could two people in two totally different stages of their lives come together? As fate would have it, Mark's sister, Glenda, had already decided the two needed to meet. The only problem was she had to convince Arlene this was a good idea.

Arlene was busy raising four girls as a single parent, not to mention she was fed up with the whole dating scene. She had sworn to the "no men rule" at least until the girls were a little older.

Mark was from Batesville and most of his family still lived in town so he would visit the area from time to time. It was on one of those trips that Glenda was able to convince Arlene to have dinner with her brother, even if it was just to get her out of the house for a few hours. Arlene was surprised at how much she and Mark had in common and how much she liked his company.

Mark decided to make the trip a bit longer than what he had initially planned so that he could see Arlene. The trips back home came more often, which Arlene thought was Mark wanting to see his family. She later found out it was her he wanted to see more of. They officially began dating in February 1984 and things escalated pretty quickly from there.

Mark and Arlene divided their time between Arkansas and Wisconsin, and many racing towns in between. They were married at the Peabody Hotel in Memphis, Tennessee, in October of 1984 and moved their family to the Charlotte, North Carolina, area soon after their wedding. However, they are now one of the few NASCAR couples who have chosen to call their permanent residence something other than Charlotte. They moved to Daytona Beach in 1994 due to the love they have for the area.

Paint Scheme

NASCAR Nextel Cup Series racing is made up of freshly painted race cars that all have their own distinct look. But remember, you can have the prettiest race car on the track, but if you don't have the other components—a fast engine or the proper setup—that pretty paint scheme will not matter. Race cars are much like people—you have to be pretty on the inside to perform pretty on the outside.

Appearance

What does your appearance say about you? Do you hold your shoulders back when you walk? Do you hold your head high? Do you look people in the eye when you talk to them? These are all personality traits that become your paint scheme. This is what others see when they see you. Sit up straight, shoulders back, and chin up. This is your chance to shine . . . shine on, baby!

Tips for Making a Race-Winning Appearance
- **Always look people in the eye.** It is an old belief that if someone cannot look you in the eye when they talk, they have something to hide.
- **Put your best foot forward.** Good posture is a sign of positive energy, self-confidence, and an overall sense of balance.
- **Keep yourself well groomed.** (More on hair and makeup in Part Six.) This means those split ends need to come off. It is better to have shorter

healthy hair than long unhealthy hair. Same goes for your hands—a manicure can pretty up even the toughest of hands.

- **Dress accordingly.** Remember you want to stand out for the right reasons. Always get the scoop on wherever you are attending and dress appropriately.
- **Use good manners.** Manners seems to be a thing of the past, but should not be. Girls who display good manners set themselves shoulders above the girls who do not. In many cases it is as simple as saying thank you, excuse me, or not interrupting someone else who is talking.

Attitude Check

How would you react to each of these situations? Answer the questions and see where your attitude ranks.

1. **You plan all week to attend your favorite driver's autograph session in your hometown. You get there one hour early to guarantee the top spot only to be told you are number fifty in line.**
   A. You pitch a fit and tell them you deserve to be at the front of the line because you are his one and only.
   B. You politely take your place in line and feel confident your smile will set you apart from everyone else.
   C. You cut in line.
   D. You pay the person first in line for their spot.

2. **You are on a date with your driver at your favorite restaurant when the waiter accidentally spills your glass of red wine on you.**
   A. You get up and sucker-punch the waiter.
   B. You politely ask for some soda water to dab your clothes.
   C. You run out of the restaurant crying.
   D. You throw your date's drink back at the waiter.

3. **You are in Victory Lane celebrating your first win as a driver's girl-friend when a motorsports photographer asks you to move out of the camera shot.**
   A. You knock the photographer's camera out of his hand.
   B. You step aside and let him take his picture but then smoothly glide back into the festivities.

C. You yell at the top of your lungs what a jerk he is.

D. You refuse and hold your spot.

4. **Another driver's girlfriend confronts you after the race to tell you how big of a jerk she thinks your boyfriend is.**

   A. You grab her by the hair and throw her to the pavement.

   B. You calmly remind her . . . *what happens on the track, stays on the track,* but you appreciate her concern.

   C. You agree and tell her you have already decided that same thing.

   D. You tell her what a jerk *she* is and to grow up.

5. **You conveniently show up at your driver's favorite restaurant the night he's there only to be told there is a forty-five-minute wait, which means by the time you are seated he will be leaving.**

   A. You grab his waiter and tie him up in the stockroom so you can take over his duties.

   B. You come back another time but a bit earlier to get a seat.

   C. You pay off the waiter to find you a table.

   D. You go to plan B, which is locking your keys in your car just as he is leaving the restaurant.

6. **Your friend invites you to a NASCAR party that your favorite driver is supposed to be at. She tells you to dress like him, which you do, only to find all the other women wearing cocktail dresses.**

   A. You demand your friend trade outfits with you—immediately!

   B. You take off the helmet, fix your hair, and laugh it off.

   C. You hide behind a potted plant miserably.

   D. You drive away from the party at 185 mph.

7. **You finally got that pit pass you always wanted and are sitting on pit road on qualifying day when he starts walking your way.**

   A. You start waving and calling his name.

   B. You calmly continue what you were doing before he came along, but glance his way and give a little smile.

   C. You run up and ask for a picture and an autograph.

   D. You pass out before he even gets to you.

8. **You are attending a race in the grandstands when the beer-drinking fan beside you decides to verbally bash your driver.**

   A. You knock him out with your purse.

   B. You ignore him.

   C. You yell back that his driver is not so great either.

   D. You start chanting your driver's name.

9. **You attend a charity event with your best friend hoping to meet your favorite driver, but when the time comes for the "chance meeting" your best friend decides it is *her* "chance meeting" with *your* guy.**

   A. You grab the hem of your long dress and take your friend down for the All American Tackle.

   B. You politely remind her why you attended the ball and calmly move back into the picture.

   C. You accidentally (yeah, whatever) spill your red wine down her dress at the most inopportune time.

   D. You find another guy for your friend so you can take center stage with yours.

10. **Your favorite driver gets engaged to someone else.**

    A. You throw the sheets over your head and never come out.

    B. You are happy for him and move on to someone else.

    C. You eat a dozen chocolate chip cookies.

    D. You cry a river.

Answer Key

Count up how many As, Bs, Cs, and Ds and see where you rank in handling life's little mishaps.

  Mostly As—Well, Ricky Bobby, you might want to read the latest Miss Manners *guide.*

  Mostly Bs—You Go Girl—Overall you are in a good place . . . your momma would be proud!

  Mostly Cs—You might want to rethink your people skills just a bit.

  Mostly Ds—You get an A for effort.

Match the Driver 2

Drivers' wives in many cases become almost as well known as their husbands. Can you match the driver to his wife?

A. Michael Waltrip   1. Krissie

B. Bobby Labonte   2. Kim

C. Kurt Busch   3. Katie

D. Jimmie Johnson   4. DeLana

E. Jeff Burton   5. Shana

F. Kevin Harvick   6. Kelley

G. Dale Jarrett   7. Eva

H. Matt Kenseth   8. Donna

I. Jeremy Mayfield   9. Chandra

J. Ryan Newman   10. Buffy

Answer Key: A-10, B-8, C-7, D-9, E-2, F-4, G-6, H-3, I-5, J-1

Pit Road Wisdom

Taking care of yourself is one of the greatest gifts you can give yourself. If you feel good on the inside, you will shine on the outside. Let it shine baby!

Part Four

The Red Flag

Whoa! Hit the brakes, girl!

He's So Not into You

Okay, girls, there does come a time in everyone's life when she has to take a reality check on who she thinks is her perfect guy. Could it be that who you think is your Mr. Right might just be someone else's Mr. Right? Guys are good at many things but hiding the fact that they are *just not into you* is not one of them. This is not to say that they cannot change their minds down the road, but for the time being we have to accept their choices— like it or not.

How to Know When He Is So Not into You

1. **He does not make eye contact.** This could mean that he does not have the desire to make contact with you at all. Some guys have problems with looking people in the eye because they are shy, but more times than not it means they are not interested . . . at least not initially.

2. **He is making eye contact with your best friend.** This is pretty much self-explanatory. If he is attempting to make contact with your friend, he might be into her and not you.

3. **He continues to look around the room when you are introduced for the first time.** Not only is this rude and disrespectful, but it certainly sends the negative message that he is not interested in what (or who) is in front of him. Basically, he is always looking for what is in the other pasture.

4. **He has a wife.** Enough said!

5. **He does not ask you your name.** If he does not care what your name is, he probably does not have much interest. When a guy asks for your

name, he wants to make a connection, even if it's just to place your face with a name.

6. **He does not introduce you to his friends.** This can mean that he does not intend to have you around much so why introduce you to his friends. It can also mean that he may somehow be embarrassed by you or your relationship. This is never a good sign.

7. **He asks you a question you've already answered.** Meaning basically that he's not interested enough to listen to you. It could, however, also mean that all the years around loud motors have impaired his hearing.

8. **He still says "nice to meet you" after you have been introduced numerous times.** Okay, what does it take to get into this guy's head? Is he just plain stupid or did you maybe not make a good impression on him any of the previous times you were introduced?

9. **He asks if you want an autograph.** The fact that he thinks you are a groupie or pit lizard is bad enough, but come on . . . get over yourself.

10. **He tries to hook you up with his crew chief.** Not a good sign! If he is attempting to set you up with someone else, it is a surefire way to know he is not on the same page as you.

11. **He never calls.** The fact that his Nextel phone works almost anywhere should basically tell you that he is so not into you. Note to self: Never call him!

12. **Date number two never comes.** This is one of the cold hard facts that everyone must learn to face when in the dating scene.

13. **He talks to you about his ex.** If he is talking about his ex (good or bad) he is thinking about her and not you. Becoming a great shoulder to lean on is not what you have in mind, even though he may.

14. **He never offers a garage pass.** If he invites you to the race but does not get you a pass for the garage, things are not so good. Basically, he wants you there but not too close.

The Top Five . . .

BOYS NEXT DOOR

1. Kasey Kahne
2. Reed Sorenson
3. Clint Bowyer
4. Jon Wood
5. David Stremme

15. **He meets you out but never picks you up for a date.** Making things too easy for him is not a good idea. What does he have to work for? If he does not respect you enough to come to your door and pick you up for a date, you should not make yourself so readily available.

16. **He asks your last name after two dates.** Ouch! Maybe you should get a name tag and wear it on your next date.

17. **He asks you for your credit card to split the dinner bill.** If he asks you to dinner, but then expects you to pay your share, he is under the assumption you are out as friends, or he had his head shook around too much in his last wreck.

18. **He never asks about you.** Not asking usually means not wanting to know.

19. **He only talks about himself.** Enough about me; let's talk about me . . . please! Who has time for self-absorbed men? Not you!

20. **He tells you if he wins the race to skip Victory Lane and wait for him in the garage area.** I don't think so, buster! That is when you throw the red flag at him and move on!

How to Spot a Pit Lizard

Pit lizards—venomous creatures even exterminators can't stomp out—have been around the sport of NASCAR racing since its inception in 1948. I have questioned whether or not some of the lizards have actually been in the garage area since 1948, but that is neither here nor there. Above all, you do not want to be labeled a pit lizard.

So what exactly is a pit lizard? This would be a blood-sucking, often hard-to-remove-from-the-skin creature that slimes her way into areas that one would not expect. She does it *without* grace, sensibility, tact, or pride. She simply attaches herself to anyone who can get her into places that are normally off limits to bottom-feeding creatures.

Why, you might ask, would such a creature still exist in an area that should be critter-free? That time-honored question has never been answered.

Tips to Spotting a Pit Lizard

1. She is the only one in the garage area wearing a tank top with cleavage displayed for all to see.
2. She somehow wiggles her Daisy Duke short-shorts past the NASCAR fashion police.
3. Her hair is bigger than a Roush engine.
4. She considers her three-inch heels normal race day attire.
5. She smacks her gum.

Girlfriend to Girlfriend

Trust me when I say . . . once a pit lizard, always a pit lizard. This is not the approach to take when trying to win your driver's heart. Most guys will tell you if they can't take them home to Momma, they don't take 'em home.

6. She often works in a team (very seldom do you see a lizard sliming solo).
7. She has a garage pass, but no team claims her as their own.
8. She slimes around a different team hauler each week.
9. She somehow finances traveling the full (or majority) of the circuit without proof of employment.
10. She gives you a nasty look when you talk to any eligible man in her vicinity.

How Not to Be One

How not to be a pit lizard is pretty easy. If you are reading this thinking, "Wow, girls really do that?" then you are probably not one.

NASCAR racing is not any different from other high-profile lifestyles in that there is always a group of girls who work hard (too hard) to put themselves in the eye of the storm. You want to make sure you handle yourself with dignity and never put yourself in a position to come across as unworthy, desperate, or loosey-goosey.

Drivers may be cute, but no one is worth trading your dignity and pride for. If you remember those things you will stay clear of the reptiles that feed off the asphalt.

Tips on How Not to Be a Pit Lizard

1. You abide by the clothing rules set forth by NASCAR.
2. You do not show your cleavage for all to see.
3. You wait to chew gum in private.
4. You only go where your credentials allow you to go.
5. You make friends, but never tread in anyone else's water—if a guy is off limits to everyone else, respect that he is off limits to you as well.
6. You understand that married means unavailable . . . period!
7. You know there is a difference between being persistent and being a pain in the tail.
8. You understand when someone is not into you.
9. You have a job.
10. The blisters from your stilettos are just not worth the trouble.

The Top Five . . .

NAMES FOR PIT LIZARDS

1. Bottom-feeders
2. Diesel sniffers
3. Germs
4. Groupies
5. Race leeches

Plastic or Paper?

This is a little secret that I divulged in *The Girl's Guide to NASCAR* which became quite a conversation piece. If you asked the drivers what it meant to be plastic or paper they had no idea what was being asked of them, but if you asked the drivers' wives . . . they knew right away.

NASCAR is very specific about who gets to go where at a racetrack. In order to be in the garage area, you have to have a garage pass; if you plan to enter pit road, you must have a pit pass; and so on. Each team is allowed a certain number of passes for their team on any given race day. These passes are made of paper and are good only for that specific day or race weekend. Basically, it serves as a temporary pass.

Each team is also given the opportunity at the beginning of each season to purchase what is referred to as a hard card that gets you anywhere you want to go at any time at a NASCAR race. These little laminated cards are quite expensive—the license has to be purchased from NASCAR and there are only a certain number of hard cards teams are allowed to have. Teams are very selective (for obvious reasons) of who owns a hard card credential.

The age-old way to tell if a driver's new flame is seri-

Girlfriend to Girlfriend

Ladies in the garage area take the hard card vs. paper situation very seriously. Almost all girls start out with paper and are over the moon when they get their hard card. One of my great friends (who was a driver's girlfriend at the time and is now a driver's wife) forgot her hard card one weekend and had to wear a paper pass. She would not leave the garage area so she would not have to display her temporary race pass. She considered the paper pass a humiliation of sorts.

ous girlfriend material is whether or not she has a hard card. All girlfriends start out with paper but hope to one day (soon) move to permanent status.

NASCAR issues many different types of passes on any given weekend. This is to try and stay on top of how many people can be at one place at one time. Sometimes that works and sometimes it does not, but the effort is there nonetheless.

Hot Pass—Allows you access to the garage area and pit road while the race is going on. Hence the name, meaning the track is hot with activity.

Cold Pass—This is good for up to one to two hours before the race begins. This basically serves as a pre-race pass, meaning cars are not on the track.

Garage One Time Walk Thru—This is one of the newer type passes NASCAR issues. This pass was developed in hopes of cutting down on the number of nonworking bodies in the garage area. This pass is good for one entrance into the garage area, meaning you cannot walk in and out whenever you choose. The only problem is that people actually stay longer knowing they cannot return once they exit.

Top Ten Mistakes Girls Make with Their Favorite Driver

Reality is that at some time or another most of us girls just kind of get off track. Some of our crazy antics can cause our guy to throw the red flag at us.

The key to getting off track is how quickly we get back in the groove. We will talk about how to get your lap back in the next chapter, but until then here are the top ten mistakes women make with their drivers:

1. **You insist he take Sundays off.** I don't think so!

2. **You complain continually about the hectic schedule of the NASCAR circuit.** This is something that will not change, and your guy has nothing to do with the schedule. Either you deal with it or put on your walking shoes.

3. **You try and tell him how to drive a race car.** What on earth would make you want to do such a thing?

4. **You become too needy.** Race car drivers are no different from most men in that your becoming too needy or not allowing them enough space is a surefire way to send them hiking.

5. **You tell race secrets to another team.** Not only are you being dishonest to your guy, but you are also leaving the door open for people to question your integrity and motives.

6. **Saturday night is your big party night.** Maybe switching to Friday would be a better option . . .

7. **You insist on your mother, grandmother, and brother coming to the races with you.** So are you planning on inviting them to a sleepover too? Leave the family unit where the family unit resides unless your guy feels otherwise.

8. **You try to change who he is.** This is not good for you or him. If you do not like the way he is . . . he is not your guy.

9. **You become a little too friendly with another driver.** No quicker way to slime into the pit lizard family.

10. **You prematurely act like you are a family.** Yikes, this is like putting fire under his tail in the complete opposite direction of where you want the relationship to go. Guys like to be the ones to make the plans and moves. You might want to tone that down a notch.

Pit Road Wisdom

Sometimes it is hard to determine if a red flag is a permanent roadblock or merely a bump in the road. Learning to trust our instincts becomes one of our most valuable tools in life. In most cases, if it feels like something is not right, it probably isn't right.

Part Five

⚙

The Black Flag

Don't give up, you're still in the race!

Staying on the Lead Lap

Have you ever noticed how your favorite driver sometimes has to battle to stay on the lead lap? There is no worse place for a driver on the track than trying to keep up. No matter how good a team and driver may be, sometimes things just don't go their way.

What makes a team championship material is doing their very best not to put themselves in position to go a lap down and, if they do, being able to quickly regroup and get back in race contention.

Tips to staying on the lead lap

1. **Go with the flow.** Going with the flow, especially in a new relationship, is the key to success. A racer's life is in the fast lane; things are always changing and moving fast. Being spontaneous and willing to accept change is a sign of flexibility and, more importantly, maturity.

2. **Think low-maintenance.** The squeaky wheel may get the grease in some cases, but not usually with men. The easier you are to have around, the more likely you are to be around . . . catch my drift?

3. **See no evil, hear no evil, speak no evil.** No one likes a mouthy know-it-all. What you see and hear is better left for your eyes and ears. A racetrack is no different from any other workplace in that rumors are spread and things get blown out of proportion due to lack of self-control. Most guys find this very unattractive.

4. **Remember who the professional race car driver is.** Don't make the mistake of trying to tell your guy how to race or what you think of other drivers' abilities (or lack thereof). Remember, he is the professional.

5. **Fix your guy's favorite meal the night before the race.** The night before the race for most guys is a time to chill out and lie back with friends and family. Many guys eat their favorite meal and hit the sack early. Preparing your guy's favorite meal is a way to show him how special he is, and it gives you the opportunity to show what you have in the kitchen . . . (or your skillful ability to order takeout!).

6. **Play the disappearing game.** As exciting as a racetrack can be for all not working, remember it is his place of business. This is where teams discuss strategy, business deals are made, and confidential conversations take place. When business talks begin or race planning gets underway, find somewhere to go if you are not a member of the team with a specific job to do.

The Top Five . . .

WAYS TO GET A BLACK FLAG

1. You call Tony Stewart "Smoke" when introduced.
2. You call a meeting with Mike Helton to discuss the rule violation handed out to your guy in the race.
3. You steal the pace car for a lap or two.
4. You slug the driver who wrecked your guy in the race.
5. You pitch a fit on pit road because a NASCAR official got in your way.

7. **Let him lead.** Call them old-fashioned, but most guys want to take the lead—whether it's asking you out on the first date or even when to hold hands. Being pushy has not been a great relationship tool for most. Backing off is a sign of self-confidence and maturity.

8. **Act composed and unaffected.** How goofy and awkward would it be for a driver to have his girl starstruck over the fact that they are standing at drivers' introduction together only minutes before the start of the race? Even if you are feeling that way, save the outburst until after you get home—or at least for the potty break. Drivers need to know you are there for them and could care less about your surroundings.

9. **Make him think he is the king of your racing world.** Even if you think Richard Petty should be enshrined in the Walk of Fame, make your guy feel like he is the one and only king of auto racing. A little white lie never hurt anyone.

10. **Be intuitive.** Knowing what your guy needs, when to encourage, when to back off, when to cheer him on, or even when to exit is one of the hardest things we girls have to do in relationships. Being intuitive will help you more than it will help him. Your intuition will always lead you in the right direction.

The Lucky Dog Pass

If you are like most, you will at some time or another go a lap down. Few of us are able to stay on the lead lap all the time. Wouldn't it be nice to have a little luck on your side . . . say maybe a Lucky Dog Pass that enables you to not only get your lap back, but also puts you right back in the heat of the race?

---

fast fact

Racing back to the yellow (flag) once a caution (flag) comes out is not allowed in NASCAR Nextel Cup Series racing. This race strategy (banned from NASCAR in 2003) enabled drivers a lap down to get back on the lead lap. Currently NASCAR gives the first car a lap down a free pass once the caution flag waves, which puts the pass recipient back on the lead lap. This free pass is also referred to as the Lucky Dog Pass.

Tips to Getting Your Lap Back

1. **Agree to disagree.** Sometimes you just have to agree to disagree. He can't be right all the time nor can you.
2. **Show him you care.** Actions speak louder than words. Show him; don't tell him.
3. **Let him be right when he's not now and then.** Sometimes you just have to treat guys like little children by laying on the reverse psychology. Tell them one thing; then do another.

4. **Don't make a mountain out of a molehill.** Why do girls always do this? Could it be that maybe he is just stressed about the race, even though you think he is stressed with you?

5. **The disappearing act.** Make like Houdini and disappear. Sometimes not being there makes guys realize how much they like having you around.

6. **Leave a sweet meaningless note in his race uniform.** This is not the time for the sappy love letter, just wishful thoughts for a safe race.

7. **Kiss his pillowcase with his favorite color lipstick.** Talk about laying it on. The last thing he will see when he throws the flag on another day are your lips. Guaranteed to make him dream about you.

8. **Don't tamper with or disable the other forty-two cars in the field.** Even though this sounds like a great idea, I would not recommend this race strategy. There has to be more than one car in the field to have a race.

9. **Make fun of yourself.** Learning to laugh at ourselves is one of the best tools to relationship building and life in general. There are many ways to lighten up, like jelly bowl laughing.

10. **Remind him that you are only human.** Not only are you only human, but so is he. Admitting our mistakes and realizing that they are a part of life is a great way to learn and grow.

Girlfriend to Girlfriend

We all do things that we wish we could take back. If your guy can't accept you even with your shortcomings, he's probably not your guy.

Getting Him Race-Ready

Most guys need a little help at times to get them moving in the right direction . . . you know, as in "race-ready." Ever heard of the Peter Pan Complex? Many psychologists believe that men are like children in that they need persuading, they want to be taken care of and nurtured, and at times can be big babies (well now that's a shocker). There are numerous studies that show men actually seek out (subconsciously) women who remind them of Mom or have similar traits to their mom's personality.

A little gentle persuading can be done in different ways, but one of the most time-tested ways to his heart is through his stomach. Have you ever noticed how your guy can be tired, worn-out, and ornery, but you cook his favorite meal and he suddenly comes to life?

Aw, guys are so predictable . . . give them home cooking and you are heading for the checkered flag.

Recipes to Race into His Heart

Preparing meals for racers is no different from cooking for any other guy, except they will probably have to miss Sunday dinner.

Many drivers' wives have their own family traditions for race wins, championship wins, and even pole positions. Some even prepare special meals for every Saturday night before the Sunday race. Drivers are different in what they like to eat the night before the race and even the morning of. Some believe racers should load up on carbs while others believe lean meats and veggies are brain foods.

Here are a few ideas for a romantic dinner sure to get you to the Victory Lane with him.

Girlfriend to Girlfriend

Davey would only eat pasta the night before a race. He not only thought it was good for his body to load up on carbs, but he was also superstitious. He thought if he didn't eat his same baked spaghetti with meatballs that Lady Luck would not shine on him for race day.

Race Meal #1

A classic Italian-inspired meal guaranteed to satisfy. This one always gets the checkered flag!

Salad—Creamy Salad

I have yet to find anyone who does not love this salad. The herbs are what make the tastebuds go wild. He will not believe you made this dressing just for him . . . even though we know you would have made it for yourself anyway.

4 cups mixed salad greens
6 sliced cherry tomatoes
¼ cup mayonnaise
1 tablespoon milk
1 tablespoon cider vinegar
½ teaspoon dried oregano
½ teaspoon dried basil
¼ teaspoon sugar
⅛ teaspoon garlic powder
⅛ teaspoon garlic salt
Black pepper to taste

Place washed greens on salad plate. Arrange tomatoes on greens. In a salad dressing jar with lid, combine the remaining ingredients and shake vigorously. Drizzle over salad.

The Top Five . . .

ITEMS IN A DRIVER'S GROCERY CART

1. Peanut butter
2. Bread
3. Bottled water
4. Protein bars
5. Popcorn

🏁 🏁 🏁 Entrée—Old-Fashioned Lasagna

I have tooled around with many lasagna recipes through the years, but none have a flavor like this one. This recipe takes the checkered flag every time I serve it.

1 pound lean ground beef
1 clove minced garlic
1 tablespoon parsley flakes
1 tablespoon basil
1½ teaspoons salt
2 cups stewed chopped tomatoes
Two 6-ounce cans tomato paste
One 8-ounce package lasagna noodles

Cheese Filling
Two 12-ounce cartons ricotta cheese
2 eggs, beaten
1 teaspoon salt
½ teaspoon pepper
2 tablespoons parsley flakes

The Top Five . . .

HEALTHY TRACK SNACKS

1. Apples
2. Pretzels
3. Nuts
4. Granola bars
5. Bananas

½ cup grated Parmesan cheese
1 pound shredded mozzarella cheese

Brown meat; slowly add in garlic, parsley, basil, salt, tomatoes, and tomato paste. Simmer uncovered for about one hour. Cook lasagna noodles according to package instructions. For the filling, combine ricotta cheese with eggs, salt, pepper, parsley, and Parmesan and set aside. Place half of the noodles in a greased 13×9×2 casserole dish. Spread one half of the cheese filling mixture over noodles, layer half of the mozzarella cheese and half of the meat sauce. Repeat layers. Bake at 375° for 30 minutes.

🏁 🏁 🏁 Dessert—Chocolate Lovers' Chocolate Mousse

This dessert is light and easy to fix. After a heavy meal, you won't have much room for anything else.

1 ½ cups whipping cream
½ cup sugar
½ cup sifted baking cocoa
½ teaspoon vanilla extract
½ teaspoon rum extract

Combine all of the ingredients in a mixing bowl. Beat until chocolate mixture is soft and fluffy. Spoon into dessert bowls. Freeze for 2 hours before serving.

Girlfriend to Girlfriend

I find it hard to make yeast rolls from scratch when you can buy them in the frozen food section of your favorite grocery just as well. My favorite is Sister Schubert's!

Race Meal #2

If you're looking to spice up the night, this flavorful meal will rev both your engines. Vroom!

🏁 🏁 🏁 Salad—Upside-Down Salad

This salad is a wonderful way to bring out the natural vibrant flavor of zucchini, olives, and red onions. I like this salad because it is just different enough to offer a new flavor but not so crazy that one would be afraid to indulge—though you'll want a mint after eating the onions.

> **2 cups shredded lettuce**
> **½ cup shredded zucchini**
> **½ cup sliced ripe olives**
> **¼ cup chopped red onion**
> **½ cup Italian dressing**
> **¼ cup shredded Parmesan cheese**

In a salad bowl, combine the lettuce, zucchini, olives, and onion. Drizzle with the dressing. Sprinkle with Parmesan cheese.

Entrée—Low-Country Shrimp Creole

Growing up in South Carolina, I was raised on fresh seafood from the coast. My grandmother used to serve this hearty meal for Sunday dinner. I would prepare this for Davey after a big race win. It was one of his favorite dishes.

The Top Five . . .
DRIVER BEVERAGES
1. Pepsi or Coke
2. Gatorade
3. Good ole water
4. Yoo-hoo
5. Red Bull

> **½ cup chopped green pepper**
> **¼ cup chopped onion**
> **1 chopped celery rib**
> **1 clove of minced garlic**
> **1½ teaspoons vegetable oil**
> **One 15-ounce jar tomato sauce**
> **1 teaspoon dried oregano**
> **1 bay leaf**
> **½ pound cooked medium shrimp, peeled and deveined**
> **1 box cooked rice**

In a skillet, sautée the green pepper, onion, celery, and garlic in oil until tender. Add the tomato sauce, oregano, and bay leaf. Reduce heat to simmer, cook uncovered for 20 minutes. Stir in shrimp and cook for 3 minutes. Discard bay leaf. Serve over rice.

🏁 🏁 🏁 Dessert—Chocolate Mint Parfaits

You will love the simplicity of this recipe. Not only is it rich and creamy, but the mint will leave you both feeling refreshed.

2 cups cold milk, divided
One 3.9-ounce package instant chocolate pudding mix
4 ounces cream cheese, softened
1 tablespoon sugar
¼ teaspoon peppermint extract
1 cup whipped topping
4 to 6 Andes mints

In a bowl, whisk milk and pudding mix for 2 minutes; set aside. In a separate bowl, beat cream cheese, sugar, and extract. Fold in whipped topping. Layer the pudding first, then cream cheese mixture, pudding, and cream cheese. Garnish with Andes mints.

Race Meal #3

If your guy likes to eat light, this combination will help him get race-ready.

🏁 🏁 🏁 Salad—Tossed Salad with a Lemon Twist

This salad is light, refreshing, and very tasty. It doesn't hurt that it is easy to prepare. This is one of my favorite standbys because it is so quick and tastes fresh and light. He will think you spent hours on your homemade dressing.

Salad greens
2 medium tomatoes cut into wedges
¾ cup sliced cucumber
½ cup vegetable oil
¼ cup lemon juice

1 clove minced garlic
1 teaspoon sugar
1 teaspoon dried oregano
Salt and pepper to taste

In a salad server, combine greens, tomatoes, and cucumber. Set aside. In a salad dressing jar with a top, combine all the remaining ingredients and shake well. Slowly drizzle dressing over greens until coated.

🏁 🏁 🏁 Entrée—To-Die-For Chicken

This is the best chicken you will ever put in your mouth or his. This recipe will leave him longing to see you (and the chicken) again.

6 chicken thighs
3 tablespoons lemon juice
2 tablespoons honey
1 tablespoon olive oil
3 cloves minced garlic
2 teaspoons dried oregano

Place the chicken in a greased 13×9×2 baking dish. In a bowl, combine the lemon juice, honey, oil, garlic, and oregano and stir. Pour the mixture over the chicken. Bake uncovered at 375° for 45 minutes. Baste the chicken every 15 minutes with the sauce in its pan.

Girlfriend to Girlfriend

Every driver is different in how he likes to celebrate a win. Some of my most special memories of Davey and our family were after he won a race. I would invite his mom and dad, his brother and sisters, and all of his friends for dinner. I always had a special cake made up with the race name and, of course, checkered flags.

🏁 🏁 🏁 Dessert—Pear and Apple Crisp

This is a dessert only his grandma could pull off, but now you have an edge up on your competition. This dessert is incredibly delicious; it will leave him feeling warm and fuzzy all over.

One 21-ounce can apple pie filling
One 8½-ounce can sliced pears, drained

½ cup packed brown sugar
½ cup all-purpose flour
¼ cup oatmeal
½ teaspoon ground cinnamon
6 tablespoons cold butter
vanilla ice cream

In a greased 9-inch baking dish, combine pie filling and pears; set aside. In a small bowl, combine brown sugar, flour, oatmeal, and cinnamon. Cut in butter until mixture resembles crumbs. Sprinkle over fruit. Bake at 350° for 25 minutes. Serve ice cream over the top of warm dessert.

Race Meal #4

Warm his belly and his toes on chilly evenings with this simple and comforting combination.

🏁 🏁 🏁 Entrée—White Chili

This is one of my family's favorite meals, especially when it is cool outside. No better way to race into his heart than with hearty chili on a cool fall day.

2 pounds cooked and cooled chicken breast
2 cups chicken stock from cooking chicken
1 tablespoon olive oil
2 chopped onions
4 cloves minced garlic
Two 4.5-ounce cans chopped green chiles
2 teaspoons ground cumin
½ teaspoon dried oregano
¼ teaspoon ground cloves
¼ teaspoon ground cayenne pepper
Six 16-ounce cans white beans
1 cup shredded Monterey Jack cheese
Black pepper to taste

Shred cooked chicken, removing skin and bones (I use boneless chicken breast). Measure reserved stock and set aside. In a large pot, heat oil. Add onions, garlic, chiles, cumin, oregano, cloves, and cayenne pepper. Stir and cook over low to medium heat for 5 to 6 minutes. Add drained beans and chicken stock. Increase heat to a boil, and then reduce heat. Simmer, covered, for 50 minutes. Add chicken and cheese, stir until cheese melts. To serve, ladle into bowls and garnish, if desired, with cheese, fresh cilantro, salsa, sour cream, and tortilla chips.

🏁 🏁 🏁 Dessert—Banana Supreme

Bananas are no stranger to the racetrack, due largely to the convenience of eating a banana on the go. This recipe will not leave him yearning for the racetrack, but it will help you earn a few extra points.

½ cup butter
1½ cups confectioner's sugar
1 tablespoon water
1 teaspoon lemon juice
1 teaspoon vanilla extract
¼ teaspoon ground cinnamon
2 cups firm bananas
vanilla bean ice cream

The Top Five . . .

WAYS TO A ROMANTIC DINNER

1. Dim the lights
2. Burn candles on the table
3. Play soft music
4. Don't talk about work
5. Place fresh flowers on the table

In a small saucepan, melt butter. Stir in sugar, water, and lemon juice until smooth. Cook over medium-low heat for 4 to 5 minutes, stirring occasionally. Remove from heat; stir in vanilla and cinnamon. Fold in bananas. Serve warm over ice cream.

Race Track Etiquette

Race car drivers have a code that you cannot find in NASCAR's rulebook. These unspoken rules were set in stone many years ago in NASCAR's elite series, and are simply referred to as the Gentleman's Agreement. They are the key do's and don'ts on the track. A driver who abides by the Gentleman's Agreement and races with integrity is known as a "clean racer," while a "dirty racer" races his competitors without thinking about the repercussions.

Similarly, there are additional rules not in the official NASCAR rulebook for pit road, the garage area, and Victory Lane. These rules sometimes take a little trial and error to figure out. Anyone who has been permitted to enter the restricted areas (including wives and girlfriends) is expected to abide by both the spoken and unspoken rules.

The Three Gentleman's Rules

1. If you are lapped traffic, give front-runners plenty of room to get by. This is imperative in the closing laps.
2. If you are a noncompetitive car or lapped traffic, do not do anything to affect the outcome of the race by blocking or challenging the race leaders.
3. Use caution when bump-drafting. Never bump-draft in a turn.

Girlfriend to Girlfriend

Many of the young-gun drivers that are coming on board have to be taught the lay of the land. The younger drivers who are hard-charging their way into the series find out real soon how important it is to abide by the Gentleman's Agreement. The veteran racers do not mind telling them (both on the track and off) what is acceptable and what is not.

Pit Road Etiquette

Pit road is one of the most stressful places you can be on race day. Everything on pit road kicks into high gear about three hours before the start of the race and does not slow down until a few hours after the checkered flag waves. Pit crew members are busy setting up shop and team members are hustling to make sure everything is done to perfection. One little slipup can mean the difference between a win or a loss.

While most people on pit road play a role in race day activities, there are certain significant others or special guests that do not necessarily have a job but have every right to be there nonetheless. Rules are in place on pit road first and foremost for safety, but also to keep things under control in what seems to be chaos.

Do's and Don'ts in the Pits

1. Don't ever enter anyone else's pit area during the race.
2. Don't touch any equipment. The crew guys are very particular about how and where things are set up. One little bump or touch could make a difference.
3. Do remember the crew guys are working. Be polite and cordial, and stay out of the way.

The Top Five...
BEST THINGS TO CONSIDER DOING ON RACE DAY

1. Actually watching the race.
2. Reading *Cosmopolitan*.
3. Map out your strategy on how to get asked out on date number two.
4. Inquire about the jacket you just have to have that a driver's wife is wearing.
5. Ponder how much longer until the race is over.

4. Do ask your guy where he wants you to watch the race from.
5. Do check out your surroundings. It is a long day . . . you will want to know where the restrooms and concessions are located.
6. Do be respectful of NASCAR officials at all times. NASCAR does not have a problem asking you or anyone else to leave if you are not abiding by the rules.
7. Don't expect anyone under eighteen (except drivers' children) to be allowed to enter pit road.
8. Don't ever question a NASCAR official on a race call.
9. Do converse politely with other drivers' wives and girlfriends, but then move on. This is not a place for socializing.
10. Don't ever approach another driver's wife or girlfriend about a race track incident that involves either your guy or hers.
11. Don't smoke!
12. Do abide by NASCAR's dress code policy.
13. Don't question crew members during the race about track activity. Remember, they have a job to do and it is not to be your play-by-play guy.
14. Do stay to yourself. The less you are seen or heard from the better.
15. Don't invite your best girlfriends for a day behind the scenes at the races. There is a time and place for everything.

Worst Ways to Get His Attention

1. Race out to the car for a quick kiss during his pit stop.
2. Radio him to ask what he might want for supper.
3. Paint your nails while sitting on the pit box to pass the time.
4. Grab the front tire during the pit stop because you can do it faster.
5. Stand on the pit box and scream at the crew for not having a good pit stop.

Garage Area Etiquette

The garage area is the eye of the storm on any given weekend. This is where deals are made, plans are executed, and dreams come true.

Each track garage area is different. Some have separate stall-like garage slips (which offers more privacy) while others have an open area where all the teams line their cars up under one roof. Each team is assigned a hauler parking spot (lined up by car owner points) and a garage working area for the car during practice and qualifying. Some garage areas (Daytona) even allow fans to purchase tickets to a designated area (Fan Walk) that allows them to watch the garage area happenings.

On the weekends, the garage area serves as a temporary office for every team on the NASCAR Nextel Cup Series circuit. While the garage area is mainly business in action, it is certainly a little more laid-back than pit road. It is not uncommon to see crew members goofing around with each other, drivers chatting with other drivers, and wives and girlfriends visiting.

Girlfriend to Girlfriend

In the years before the drivers had the drivers' compound area, the garage area was about the only place a driver's wife would see the other driver's wives. On Sunday morning before the race, the wives would visit and catch up on each other's lives.

Do's and Don'ts in the Garage Area

1. Do pay attention to your surroundings. This can be a dangerous place, with cars moving quickly through the garage area, especially during practice and qualifying.

2. Don't cross from one side of the garage area to the other without doing what Momma always told us . . . *stop, look, and listen!*

3. Don't bring anyone under eighteen, unless he or she is the driver's child.

4. Don't lay your purse in the line of fire—keep it on your shoulder or somewhere out of the way.

5. Don't bother your guy if he is talking to the crew.

6. Do sit back and enjoy watching all the hustle and bustle.

7. Do find a place to sit that is out of the way of foot traffic around your guy's hauler.

8. Don't consume alcoholic beverages.

9. Do offer encouraging words to your guy if he had a bad qualifying run.

10. Don't try to tell the crew how to make the car faster.

Worst Things to Do in the Garage Area

1. Get mad because your guy is talking to his crew chief more than you.

2. Insist he get done with practice in time for the 7:00 movie.

3. Hang out at another driver's hauler because he qualified better.

4. Inform your guy's car owner that he needs Atlanta race weekend off because you have a family reunion.

5. Tell your guy what you plan to do with the bonus he just received for grabbing the pole position.

Drivers' Compound Etiquette

The drivers' compound is basically a home away from home; a neighborhood of sorts for the drivers and their families. The coaches are only a few feet apart, so it's a bit like Peyton Place—nothing is kept secret here, period!

The compound is a secured area (usually located directly behind the garage area for quick and easy access) where all the drivers' motor coaches are housed. The motor coaches are lined up in rows and tucked tightly together.

The drivers live in their motor coaches when they are at the racetrack, so they're equipped with many of the modern conveniences and comforts of home, such as big-screen TVs, computers, and pumped-up stereo systems. Remember, during the race season the guys spend more time in the motor coach than their primary residence.

WAYS TO BE A NUISANCE IN THE DRIVERS' COMPOUND

1. Ask his motor coach driver to fix you your favorite lunch.
2. Knock on Jeff Gordon's coach to ask for an autograph for your dad.
3. Bring in four suitcases to stay for a while.
4. Ask him to take pictures of you in the coach for your hope chest.
5. Ask your guy to talk to your best friend on the phone so she knows you are really there.

Do's and Don'ts in the Drivers' Compound

1. Don't invite yourself to his motor coach.
2. Don't overstay your welcome.
3. Do enjoy having a place to get out of the heat.
4. Don't gawk at the other drivers . . . this is their safe haven at the track.
5. Do clean up after yourself.
6. Don't expect his coach driver to wait on you.
7. Don't use the potty in the coach . . . quietly take a stroll and find the nearest track potty.
8. Don't be overly chatty on race day . . . let him take the lead, as each driver handles race day differently.
9. Do keep to yourself and stay low-key.
10. Don't invite your family or friends to hang out in his coach with you.

Drivers' Intro Etiquette

If a driver invites you to attend drivers' introduction with him and then walk him to his car before the start of the race . . . *things are looking good for you, girl.*

All of the drivers are to report to drivers' intro about thirty to forty-five minutes before the start of the race. Each driver is introduced to the race fans in attendance and fans watching at home. The drivers are introduced by their starting order from the worst starting position (forty-third) to first.

This is one of the most highly visible places a driver can take his girlfriend or wife. Not only are all of the fans paying close attention to the drivers, but the drivers are all packed into one tight holding place waiting for their names to be called. Eyebrows are raised when a driver shows up at drivers' intro with a new girl on his arm.

Do's and Don'ts at Drivers' Intro

1. Don't invite yourself; he will ask when he is ready.
2. Do remember the three Cs . . . cool, calm, and collected.
3. Do keep to yourself.
4. Don't try to make friends with all of the drivers' wives and girlfriends . . . that will come over time.
5. Don't tell another driver he was your first pick.

The Top Five . . .
BEST TIMES TO KISS HIM ON RACE DAY

1. After breakfast before the race day mayhem starts.
2. After he straps into his car before the start of the race.
3. After the race, no matter where he finishes.
4. At your doorstep when he takes you home after a great date weekend.
5. In Victory Lane, of course!

Things *Not* to Do When He Invites you to Drivers' Intro

1. Walk across the stage with him.
2. Lay a deadlock kiss on him before he is introduced.
3. Tell him to win because you want to see what Victory Lane is like.
4. Run up and ask your dad's favorite driver, Dale Jarrett, for a picture.
5. Introduce yourself to all of the drivers' wives and tell them you will see them next week.

Victory Lane Etiquette

Victory Lane is the most exciting place to be at a racetrack. It is also the most visible place a driver can be. Once a driver wins a race and enters Victory Lane, the TV cameras start rolling and the reporters' cameras are flashing for what seems to be an eternity.

The Victory Lane celebration is centered on the driver, but a big part of the celebration is the team members, car owner, sponsor reps, driver's family and friends, and certainly his wife or girlfriend. When a driver shows up in Victory Lane with a new girl on his arm, the tongues start flapping. Everyone wants to know . . . *who's that girl?*

How They Met

CINDY AND BILL ELLIOTT

Cindy Karam was no stranger to racing when she met her future husband in 1988. In fact, she was traveling the NASCAR Cup Series circuit every weekend as a staff photographer for *Winston Cup Scene*. Bill and Cindy got to know each other casually then, but it wasn't until years later that the two would realize the attraction they had for one another.

Bill and Cindy became friends and would often hang out with each other at races and even sometimes during the week between race events, despite the fact that he lived in north Georgia and she lived in North Carolina.

It was not until an off-season ski trip to Aspen, Colorado, in 1992 that the two realized they had become more than friends. Cindy and Bill kept their relationship under wraps for a while, as she was still working for the *Scene* (and not sure how dating a driver would be perceived by her colleagues) and he had recently gone through a divorce and did not want to bring a lot of attention to the relationship out of respect for Cindy.

Near the end of the 1992 race season, Bill decided that Cindy was the one he wanted to spend the rest of his life with. In a Bill Elliott kind of way, he casually mentioned to her that he wanted to get married. The two wasted no time in making it official, and held their wedding in Blairsville, Georgia, on December 12, 1992.

Cindy continued to work as a staff photographer until the end of the 1992 season. It was during a Victory Lane celebration in November of 1992 at Atlanta Motor Speedway when she realized maybe she should be on the other side of the lens. Bill won the Cup race and was doing what all winning drivers do, which is smile for the camera. Cindy was doing what all photographers do, which is stand in the photographers pool to snap photos of the winning driver. Bill hollered for her to come get in a picture with him. She put down her camera right then and there from a professional standpoint, and has stayed on the receiving end of the camera lens ever since.

Do's and Don'ts in Victory Lane

Girlfriend to Girlfriend

Race car drivers are so funny in that they do not want you to seem interested in the cameras. If they think you are looking to get in the picture, they will think twice about why you are there.

1. Do wait to be invited . . . pushing for a more visible spot will get you a lap down.
2. Do wait for him to pull you into the photographs.
3. Don't make a big deal out of being there.
4. Do, as always, remember the three Cs . . . cool, calm, and collected.
5. Don't talk to reporters.
6. Don't chew gum, just in case the cameras are rolling.
7. Do make him believe he is king of the hill, if only for the day.

8. Don't look at your watch to see when it will be over.
9. Don't look for the cameras.
10. Do congratulate the team.

WORST THINGS TO DO IN VICTORY LANE

1. Ask the *NASCAR Scene* reporter if he would like an interview with you.
2. Show your hard card to the TV cameras.
3. Ask the crew chief not to get between you and the camera.
4. Mouth to the TV camera "He's mine!"
5. Stop the team shot so you can reapply lipstick.

Meet the Parents

If there is ever one thing that could cause the red flag to be thrown it would be meeting the parents. This is when you get the chance to see what life is really like in the fast lane . . . be it good or bad. Most race car drivers are raised in and around racing, making them race brats, and their parents, well, let's just say are the parents of the race brat. With the explosion of younger drivers coming into the sport, more and more parents are traveling the circuit week in and week out with their sons. They are there not only for moral support, but to oversee everything that goes on in his life . . . basically keeping a watchful eye.

A girl who just happens to be raised in racing herself certainly has the advantage over the ladies who were not, although sometimes ignorance is bliss! In order to make a good impression on his parents, you must first understand their way of life. Basically, you must put yourself in serious race mode. Pull those seat belts tight once more, ladies, because you are going to need them.

The Top Five . . .
WAYS TO KEEP HIS MOMMA HAPPY

1. Let him sleep single in a double bed.
2. Don't ask to take her place on the pit box.
3. Remember who was there first.
4. Ask her opinion, even when you don't want it.
5. Invite her to lunch.

What You Should Know About Racing Families

- Most families live, breathe, and sleep racing—that is all they talk about.
- Your guy just happens to be the center of their racing universe.
- Most parents have sacrificed for years for their son to be in the position he is.

- His parents go to most of the races.
- He supports the entire family financially.
- Momma sits on the pit box.
- Momma gets a new car every year.
- Weddings, birthdays, and family reunions revolve around the NASCAR schedule.
- Racing is a lifestyle-driven sport, meaning his family is very much a part of what he does.
- Family members are also employees, running everything from fan clubs to business affairs, and some even serve as crew members.

How They Met

DeLana and Kevin Harvick

DeLana was no stranger to the racetrack when she met her future husband at Southern National Raceway Park in 1999. Growing up the daughter of a racer, John Paul Linville, she knew the track ropes. She also knew how to deal with race car drivers. She had been around them her entire life.

Growing up a race brat in North Carolina had helped plant a seed for racing in her soul. At one point, DeLana even raced Late Models at Southern National Raceway Park in Kenly, North Carolina, before switching careers to the media end of the business. It was that move that brought her and Kevin together.

DeLana landed a job in the NASCAR Busch Series as a public relations rep for Randy LaJoie. During her tenure with the team, she would frequently stop by the RCR (Richard Childress Racing) truck series team hauler to see her childhood friend Todd Berrier, who just happened to be Kevin's crew chief.

DeLana and Kevin were officially introduced at drivers' introduction for the NASCAR Craftsman Truck Series event that was about to take place. He was introduced to DeLana as the next racing superstar. She took the comment with the proverbial grain of salt but took note nonetheless.

Sparks did not ignite until the two were brought together, as fate would have it, by an RCR team Christmas party. Being the good friend that she was to Todd, she agreed to be his date for the Christmas party since he did not have one. The only problem was she had a friend in town. Todd solved the issue by suggesting her friend go with Kevin, who also did not have a date.

The night didn't exactly go off without a hitch, but DeLana and Kevin found that they had a connection and a strong one at that. It was from that night on that DeLana and Kevin knew they were meant to be together.

Kevin and DeLana were married February 28, 2001, just two short weeks after Kevin was selected to fill the seat of the late great Dale Earnhardt Sr., who had tragically lost his life in a last-lap accident in the 2001 season opener, Daytona 500.

Kevin and DeLana are one of the busiest racing couples on the circuit, as Kevin drives full-time for RCR in the Cup Series, but it is what they do on the side that has impressed even the hardest cynic. Kevin and DeLana are winning car owners in the NASCAR Craftsman Truck Series and the NASCAR Busch Series on top of running Kevin Harvick, Incorporated.

It's a Family Affair

Racing just kind of has its way of running through the family. Many racers came from racers, and they often have siblings that race. Some would argue that racing is genetic, being passed down from one generation to the other. Whatever the reason, it is common to have brothers racing brothers, which also means your future brother-in-law could be the one that just took your guy out of the race . . . ouch!

On the other hand, having a built-in support system at the track is something not to be taken lightly. Kim and Donna Labonte (wives of Terry and Bobby) have enjoyed a long and supportive friendship for many years at the racetrack. Their husbands both raced on the NASCAR Nextel circuit full-time until Terry decided to trim back his schedule in 2004 to run the series part-time, which he did until 2006, when he turned in the driver's gloves for good.

Racing also goes through growing spells where some more well-known racing names seem to disappear, then all of a sudden they pop out of nowhere. This is because as racers start their own families, their kids have to be at least eighteen before they can hit the NASCAR touring track. Sometimes the age difference works out to where they can race on the track with their dads, while others never accomplish that dream due to the

The Top Five . . .
THINGS NOT TO SAY AT THE DINNER TABLE

1. Why is it that all the talent went to my guy?
2. So, planning on retiring from competition anytime soon?
3. Don't you think it is about time you let your brother win?
4. Hey, you nondriving knucklehead, could you pass the potatoes?
5. I need a little less family time . . . could you guys take the next race off?

many years between dad and son. For example, Mark Martin is pushing fifty and looking at retirement head-on. His son Matt, who is fifteen, has high hopes of making it to the Cup Series level one day, but the age difference makes it almost impossible for the two to be competitors, at least in the Cup Series.

It used to be common to have father and son on the track as fellow competitors. Richard Petty raced his son Kyle for many years, as did Bobby and Davey Allison. In fact, Bobby and Davey finished first and second in the 1988 Daytona 500. And who could forget the look of pride on Dale Earnhardt Sr.'s face in April 2000 at Texas Motor Speedway when Dale Jr. won his first Cup event?

The father-son scenario is one that may be a thing of the past in NASCAR Nextel Cup Series racing. Many believe the fact that racers are waiting later to start families is the key to the lack of father-son racing we see in the Nextel Cup Series.

In a nutshell, having brothers racing brothers or fathers racing sons can be a good thing . . . and sometimes not such a good thing; it all depends on who's out front.

Pit Road Wisdom

Getting off the pace and even crashing are things that race car drivers face every weekend in NASCAR Nextel Cup Series racing. Relationships, like races, aren't always full of chart-topping moments. Sometimes you win and sometimes you crash . . . it's how fast you get back in the race that matters.

Part Six

The White Flag

Just one lap to go!

The Chase Is On

When the white flag waves on race day, the race is nearing its end and the checkered flag is in sight. Sometimes it is hard to determine who is really racing who. In many cases the car out front (or the leader) is not the one that wins the race. It is all about control, strategy, a little bit of Lady Luck, and a whole lot of fate.

Where a relationship is going is not always so obvious to the ones watching from afar, or even to the ones in the relationship. There is one thing for sure, if you get to the white flag and you can see the checkered flag, you are further along than most. So take it for what it is worth and put the pedal to the metal, sister. There is only one race winner, and who better than you to take the win?

The Top Five . . .
PICK-ME-UPS WHEN HE HAS HAD A BAD RACE

1. "You really are the best driver ever, honey . . . really you are."
2. "All the drivers should be as good as you."
3. "No one can make the moves on the track like you."
4. "He only wishes he could drive like you."
5. "You are always my champion."

Who's Chasing Who

Racing is all about chasing each other around the track—or better yet, being chased. Relationships are no different. The dating scene is all about cat-and-mouse, but the important thing to know is when to chase and when to be chased.

Tips on How to Make Him Chase You

1. **Act like you care but not too much.** Being too needy is never a good thing.
2. **Do not return his calls right away.** You are simply letting him know that you are not sitting with one hand on the receiver and the other holding his picture.
3. **Continue to do things with your friends.** Friends are one of life's greatest gifts. Dropping friends for a guy (even a husband) is hazardous to your health. Besides, girl trips always come in handy when you have had your fill of racing and want a weekend off.
4. **Stay on course with your own goals.** Never lose sight of who you are and what you want out of life. You can be there with him as he reaches his goals and lives out his dreams, but he needs to do the same for you.
5. **Do not quit work until you are sporting an engagement ring.** Not only is this wise from a financial stand-

Girlfriend to Girlfriend

Okay, ladies, who would you want to go to the prom with? Someone who doesn't have a date, or that special someone everyone wants? Guys need a little cat-and-mouse to keep them on their toes, especially racers who are used to women throwing themselves at their feet.

point, but you are also letting him know that you can take care of yourself financially.

6. **Let him know he is important, but so are other things in your life.** Racers have a tendency to be made king of the hill by the people around them—from media reps to business managers and everyone in between. A gentle reminder that while you think he is pretty wonderful, so are other things (and people) in your life, is not only good for you, but for him as well, as it helps keep him grounded.

7. **Stay home from a race every now and then.** Showing him that you are okay with leaving the spotlight and fast-paced living aside for a weekend every now and then can be healthy for a racing relationship. It not only gives you a break, but it reminds him how much he likes you being there.

8. **Be very cool about his high-profile lifestyle.** Racers have a keen eye when it comes to girls being with them for the wrong reason. Always keeping your cool only solidifies that you are there for him and not all that goes with him.

9. **If he loves beer and you love wine, keep drinking wine.** Just because he likes something doesn't mean you have to as well. If the fact that you like wine turns him off, you were not in the race anyway.

10. **Keep a nonchalant attitude about the relationship.** This attitude drives guys crazy. Why (they wonder) can he not totally get to you? It makes them want to have you more.

The Top Five . . .
WAYS TO STOP HIM FROM CHASING YOU

1. You celebrate your first kiss by doing a burnout in his front yard.
2. You celebrate a race win by inviting his team over for a party where you serve Miller Lite when he drove the Budweiser Chevy to Victory Lane.
3. You show him his car number tattooed on your ankle with the word "forever" beside it.
4. You make comments to the *National Enquirer* about your relationship.
5. You get mad when he wins the race and thanks his primary sponsor before you.

How They Met

ANDREA AND JOE NEMECHEK

Andrea's father, Frank Blackyard, had known Joe's family for thirty years and had watched Joe grow up. It had occurred to him on several occasions that setting up his daughter with the son of his good friends would be a good idea, but it never seemed to work out.

Andrea grew up in Myrtle Beach, South Carolina, and went on to attend the University of South Carolina where she majored in retail management. It was not until after she graduated in 1988 and had landed her first job in Orlando, Florida, that she and Joe met.

In November of 1988, Andrea looked forward to attending a charity event in Orlando that her father was very involved with. It just so happened that Joe was in attendance as well. The two hit it off right from the start. Joe, who was racing Late Models in neighboring Lakeland at the time, decided to stay over an extra night so that he could have dinner with the girl who would become his wife.

The two started a long-distance relationship as she stayed in Orlando to pursue her career and he remained in Lakeland until he got the call to move to North Carolina to join a race team. They continued the long-distance relationship until he asked her to marry him in 1990. Not only did she say yes, but she packed up her bags and moved to North Carolina to be closer to her future husband.

After their wedding, on November 21, 1992, in Lakeland, Florida, Andrea and Joe settled into their racing life together in Charlotte.

Keeping It Real in the Fast Lane

I f there is one thing professional race car drivers have, it's lots of people pulling at them from many different angles. Racers have to learn to wear many hats to survive in the sport that has now become a big business. Keeping up with all the demands is not only difficult but stressful, to say the very least.

Race car drivers have the tendency to use 90 percent of their waking hours thinking about racing. The most successful race car drivers have long since figured out that racing is racing, but keeping life real is the key to success. In order for a relationship not only to survive, but to blossom in the crazy racing life, one has to commit to breaking the stress level by doing other things.

Tips on Keeping It Real

1. Plan one date night a week away from the racing life.
2. Make a pact not to discuss racing while out on your date.
3. Plan a little midweek escape at home by not answering the phone or checking e-mails for twenty-four hours.
4. Schedule a massage for two.
5. Take a walk together.
6. Go see a movie.

Girlfriend to Girlfriend

D avey and I loved to load up the kids and head to Davey's uncle's farm to get away from the fast-paced racing life. Just the way the air smelled when we got out of the car was a perfect way for us to recharge our batteries.

7. Invite some nonracing friends over for dinner.
8. Take up golf.
9. Go to see an elderly family member.
10. Attend a church service together.

The Lay of the Land

Understanding the lay of the land at a NASCAR Nextel Cup Series event is a little tricky in that every race track is different. While every track has a different track layout, the core areas of the body of the track are the same.

You can expect the following from every race track on the Cup Series circuit:

■ **Garage area:** A restricted area where the race cars are kept and worked on throughout race weekend. A Hot Pass or a One Time Walk Thru pass is needed to enter this area.

■ **Garage area sign-in:** Some tracks allow guests to pick up their Hot Passes at credentials sign-in (see below), while others direct guests to pick up their Hot Passes at the garage area sign-in. This small office is usually located at the main entrance of the garage area and is manned by a NASCAR official/employee. You will be asked to show proper ID, and you will also be required to sign a form releasing NASCAR from any accident or harm you may receive by entering the designated area.

■ **Infield:** The area found within the race loop. Some infields allow fans to purchase infield passes to camp over race weekend. The downside is that very little of the race can be seen from the infield.

■ **Pit road:** The road where pit crews service their cars during the race. Pit road can be located on the front and back straightaway of a track, depending on the size of the track surface. For example, Talladega only has one pit road due to its two-and-a-half-mile surface, while Bristol, which is a half-mile track, has to have two pit roads, one on the front stretch and one on the back stretch.

- **NASCAR hauler:** Located directly inside the garage area, this is where the drivers must sign in on the first day of practice. This is also where you can usually find Mike Helton, John Darby, and other NASCAR officials. If a driver is summoned to the trailer, he is being summoned to this spot.

- **Team haulers:** All of the teams have eighteen-wheelers to transport the race cars from one track to another. The trailers are parked inside the garage area and are used as a temporary meeting place for each team. The haulers are lined up one right after another. The cars are lined up by car owner points, meaning the driver leading the points will be the first hauler in line.

- **Driver motor coach compound:** This is a secured area where the drivers' million-dollar coaches are housed during race weekend. Most of the drivers stay in their motor coaches instead of a nearby hotel.

- **MRO trailer:** Motor Racing Outreach is a nondenominational ministry that travels with the NASCAR Nextel Cup Series. MRO provides everything from Christian counseling to child care for the drivers, team members, and their families. The MRO trailer is located inside the drivers' compound.

- **Infield care center:** Basically a temporary hospital/trauma unit set up for race weekends. The medical staff is made up of physicians, nurses, and medical specialists that provide care to anyone (including drivers) who needs immediate medical assistance.

- **Media center:** This is a building usually found near the garage area where all of the media members have quick access to the teams and any news that may be breaking in the sport. The building provides workspace for all working media, including TV, radio, and print. A special pass is required for entry.

- **Credentials sign-in:** This building is located in a different place at every track outside the race track surface, and sometimes can be hard to find. If you are a guest of someone who has signed you up for anything other than a grandstand ticket, you will need to find this office. A track official or parking attendant can usually direct you. Proper ID will be necessary as will your signature on a release form.

- **Grandstands:** Where everyone with race tickets sits.

Girlfriend to Girlfriend

More media attention is given to the drivers who are in the championship run than the nonchampionship drivers. It is not uncommon for a nonchampionship driver to win the Ford 400 but receive little media coverage after the event due to the media covering the new series champion.

- **Suites:** The suites are invitation-only and are located high above the grandstand seating. The suites are set up with stadium seating and windows from the floor to the ceiling to provide the best view. Suites are where sponsors, car owners, NASCAR officials, and track owners house their VIP guests.
- **Expo Row:** The ultimate NASCAR fan shopping experience, where all of the drivers' souvenir haulers are set up to sell merchandise. Expo Row is usually located near the main entrance of the grandstands.
- **Track offices:** Where all the track employees (including the track president) have their office space. It is usually located on the outside of the race track loop.
- **First-aid:** First-aid centers can be found in numerous places around the track, and are set up for minor and non-life-threatening issues. Anything serious or life-threatening will be directed to the infield care center or a nearby hospital. Both the first-aid centers and the infield care center are for anyone at the track, meaning race fans or race car drivers.

While understanding the lay of the land is certainly important, so is knowing who the faces are of the people you will see each week at the track.

- **Car owners:** The owners of the race cars are almost always at the racetrack, at least on race day. Owners like Jack Roush don't mind getting their hands dirty, which means it's not uncommon to find Jack under the hood of one of his race cars. Most car owners have their own motor coaches and some bring along their families.
- **Drivers:** Well, let's hope they show up or there wouldn't be much going on at a racetrack. Besides, how much fun would a racetrack be without cute boys in uniform?
- **Crew members:** This group makes up the biggest part of the NASCAR population. Every team has at least a dozen guys (at the minimum) with them at the racetrack every week. The team expands even more on race day as some of the crew fly in early race day morning and fly back out after the race is complete.
- **Sponsor reps:** You will normally see sponsor reps for the primary sponsors of the cars as well as series sponsors (Nextel, Coke, Pepsi, and so on). These reps handle any press opportunities that may come along for their product as well as take care of any company VIPs or guests.

Did You Know. . .

A driver must be at least eighteen years of age to compete in a NASCAR event.

■ **Drivers' families:** Most of the drivers like having family or friends along with them on the road. It can be pretty boring at a racetrack week in and week out without some loved ones or buddies along. The married drivers usually have their wife and kids, while the single guys either have girlfriends, siblings, or buddies to help pass the time.

■ **TV and radio crews:** The TV and radio crews are much bigger than one would expect. There may be just a few faces you see or voices you hear on the weekly coverage, but there are many folks behind the scenes that make it all happen—camera guys, setup crew, engineers, producers, and many others.

■ **Safety personnel:** The safety personnel are provided by the host city, so the faces are not the same but these crews are always there. The only exception to that would be NASCAR's safety liaison, who travels with the series week in and week out to give the drivers and their families the reassurance that someone knows their health record. It also gives the drivers a familiar face in the infield care center in case an accident should occur.

■ **Track personnel and security officers:** The track personnel and security officers are not employed by NASCAR but are there to help police the event.

■ **NASCAR officials:** NASCAR officials can be seen inside the race loop, often in the pit road and the garage area. They are easily spotted as they wear NASCAR uniforms. They help police the teams working on their cars as well as follow through with any race penalties issued during the race.

How They Met

ANN AND KENNY SCHRADER

Kenny and Ann didn't have the classic beginning of a relationship. But the people that know them best think their less-than-ordinary meeting of the hearts was quite the norm for Kenny and Ann.

The couple first met when they were married to other people. In fact, the two couples were best friends and did everything together. Both Kenny and Ann's first husband raced together at a local track in St. Louis. When Kenny and his wife separated and later divorced, Ann and her husband invited Kenny to do things with them and hang out together at the racetrack.

It was not until the demise of Ann's first marriage that she and Kenny realized they had more in common than they thought, and that they enjoyed their time together—although it did take a little convincing on both ends that they were meant to be together. Kenny continued to date around and Ann stayed unattached. During the 1981 Christmas season, Kenny was in need of a date to a racing banquet and Ann needed a date to a Christmas party so they agreed to be each other's date for each event. It was during that Christmas season that sparks flew and their relationship went to a new level.

For the next two years, Kenny and Ann dated seriously until one day Kenny decided they needed to part ways. After two short weeks, the two were reunited and looking to the future. Ann was not willing to wait for Kenny to pop the question so she did it herself, in a way that only Ann could pull off. She grabbed a calendar and told Kenny to pick a day or they were done. He picked November 13, 1984, and they were married in St. Louis.

In the early years of their marriage, Ann worked as a registered nurse during the week but would find her way to wherever Kenny was racing on the weekends. In 1986, the two moved to North Carolina as Kenny's racing career took off.

Oh, the Places We'll Go

The NASCAR Nextel Cup Series schedule consists of twenty-two different venues (tracks) spread across the country. One of the greatest things about traveling with the circuit (as a wife or girlfriend) is the opportunity to visit each of the unique host sites. Some are large metropolitan cities while others are quaint towns that add a touch of yesterday to the mix. Some of the tracks host two races a year and some are only allotted one event.

Many of the drivers' wives and girlfriends venture away from the track over the course of the weekend to see the countryside, do a little shopping, or grab a bite to eat. Knowing where your stops are on the circuit and what each track dishes out to the drivers is not only helpful for you, but it also shows your guy you care about him and the race at hand.

What You Need to Know About the Tracks

Key:

City: Where the track is located.

Inaugural year: The first year a Cup event was run at that venue.

Race date(s): The month(s) of the year that the track hosts NASCAR Nextel Cup Series event(s).

Size of track: The size of the track surface, which varies from track to track.

Shopping potential: Shopping is rated on the following scale:

    8–10—Awesome shopping—credit card alert!

    6–7—Exciting but nothing to write home about

    3–5—Better than sitting in the motor coach or hotel room for another hour

    Below 3—Don't bother!

Who's hot: A listing of drivers that have consistently performed well at the specific track.

Atlanta Motor Speedway

City: Hampton, Georgia

Inaugural year: 1960

Race dates: March and October

Size of track: 1.54 miles

Shopping potential: 10

Who's hot: Carl Edwards, Jimmie Johnson, Jeff Gordon, Bobby Labonte, Kevin Harvick, Dale Earnhardt Jr.

Bristol Motor Speedway

City: Bristol, Tennessee

Inaugural year: 1961

Race dates: April and August

Size of track: .533 mile

Shopping potential: 2

Who's hot: Kurt Busch, Tony Stewart, Elliott Sadler, Dale Earnhardt Jr., Jeff Gordon

California Speedway

City: Fontana, California

Inaugural year: 1997

Race dates: February and September

Size of track: 2 miles

Shopping potential: 10

Who's hot: Jeff Gordon, Elliott Sadler, Kurt Busch, Jimmie Johnson

Chicagoland Speedway

City: Joliet, Illinois

Inaugural year: 2001

> ## The Top Five...
> ### BEST SHOPPING TRACKS
> 1. Atlanta
> 2. California
> 3. Homestead-Miami
> 4. Infineon
> 5. Phoenix

Did You Know...

The Bristol night race is considered the hottest (and hardest) ticket to acquire.

Race date: July
Size of track: 1.5 miles
Shopping potential: 4
Who's hot: Kevin Harvick, Ryan Newman, Tony Stewart

Darlington Raceway
City: Darlington, South Carolina
Inaugural year: 1950
Race date: May
Size of track: 1.366 miles
Shopping potential: 2
Who's hot: Jeff Burton, Jeff Gordon, Jimmie Johnson, Sterling Marlin, Dale Jarrett

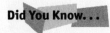

Did You Know...

After winning at the Brickyard, the driver and his team members (as well as his significant other) kiss the bricks— the Kodak moment of the event.

Daytona International Speedway
City: Daytona Beach, Florida
Inaugural year: 1959
Race dates: February and July
Size of track: 2.5 miles
Shopping potential: 5
Who's hot: Dale Earnhardt Jr., Jeff Gordon, Tony Stewart, Jeff Burton, Greg Biffle, Michael Waltrip, Dale Jarrett

Dover International Speedway
City: Dover, Delaware
Inaugural year: 1969
Race dates: June and September
Size of track: 1 mile
Shopping potential: 6
Who's hot: Ryan Newman, Tony Stewart, Jeff Gordon, Dale Earnhardt Jr., Jimmie Johnson

Homestead-Miami Speedway
City: Homestead, Florida
Inaugural year: 1995
Race date: November
Size of track: 1.5 miles

Shopping potential: 10

Who's hot: Tony Stewart, Greg Biffle, Kurt Busch, Bobby Labonte

Indianapolis Motor Speedway

City: Indianapolis, Indiana

Inaugural year: 1994

Race date: July

Size of track: 2.5 miles

Shopping potential: 7

Who's hot: Jimmie Johnson, Kevin Harvick, Jeff Gordon, Dale Jarrett, Bobby Labonte

Infineon Raceway

City: Sonoma, California

Inaugural year: 1989

Race date: June

Size of track: 1.99 miles road course

Shopping potential: 10

Who's hot: Kevin Harvick, Jeff Gordon, Robby Gordon, Tony Stewart

Kansas Speedway

City: Kansas City, Kansas

Inaugural year: 2001

Race date: October

Size of track: 1.5 miles

Shopping potential: 6

Who's hot: Ryan Newman, Jeff Gordon, Joe Nemechek

Las Vegas Motor Speedway

City: Las Vegas, Nevada

Inaugural year: 1998

Race date: March

Size of track: 1.5 miles

Shopping potential: 10

Who's hot: Matt Kenseth, Jeff Burton, Jeff Gordon

The Top Five...

BEST SENSE OF HUMOR

1. Clint Bowyer
2. Casey Mears
3. Carl Edwards
4. David Stremme
5. Elliott Sadler

Lowe's Motor Speedway

City: Concord (near Charlotte), North Carolina
Inaugural year: 1960
Race dates: May and October
Size of track: 1.5 miles
Shopping potential: 10
Who's hot: Jimmie Johnson, Tony Stewart, Matt Kenseth, Jamie McMurray, Jeff Burton, Jeff Gordon

Martinsville Speedway

City: Martinsville, Virginia
Inaugural year: 1956
Race dates: April and October
Size of track: .526 mile
Shopping potential: 2
Who's hot: Jimmie Johnson, Jeff Gordon, Kurt Busch, Tony Stewart

Michigan International Speedway

City: Brooklyn, Michigan
Inaugural year: 1969
Race dates: June and August
Size of track: 2 miles
Shopping potential: 5
Who's hot: Greg Biffle, Tony Stewart, Jeff Gordon, Kurt Busch, Matt Kenseth, Dale Jarrett

New Hampshire International Speedway

City: Loudon, New Hampshire
Inaugural year: 1993
Race dates: July and September
Size of track: 1.058 miles
Shopping potential: 2
Who's hot: Jimmie Johnson, Jeff Burton, Jeff Gordon, Tony Stewart, Robby Gordon

Phoenix International Raceway

City: Avondale, Arizona
Inaugural year: 1988

Race dates: April and November
Size of track: 1 mile
Shopping potential: 10
Who's hot: Matt Kenseth, Jeff Burton, Dale Earnhardt Jr., Tony Stewart

Pocono Raceway
City: Long Pond, Pennsylvania
Inaugural year: 1974
Race dates: June and July
Size of track: 2.5 miles
Shopping potential: 3
Who's hot: Jimmie Johnson, Jeremy Mayfield, Tony Stewart, Denny Hamlin, Jeff Gordon, Carl Edwards

Richmond International Raceway
City: Richmond, Virginia
Inaugural year: 1953
Race dates: May and September
Size of track: .75 mile
Shopping potential: 9
Who's hot: Dale Earnhardt Jr., Tony Stewart, Kasey Kahne, Jeff Gordon, Mark Martin

Talladega Superspeedway
City: Talladega, Alabama
Inaugural year: 1969
Race dates: April and October
Size of track: 2.66 miles
Shopping potential: 1
Who's hot: Dale Earnhardt Jr., Michael Waltrip, Jeff Gordon, Tony Stewart

Texas Motor Speedway
City: Fort Worth, Texas
Inaugural year: 1997
Race dates: April and November
Size of track: 1.5 miles
Shopping potential: 7
Who's hot: Elliott Sadler, Dale Earnhardt Jr., Jeff Burton, Matt Kenseth, Ryan Newman, Kasey Kahne

Very few of the drivers like road course racing. The majority of the drivers feel the road courses have no place in NASCAR Nextel Cup Series racing.

Watkins Glen International

City: Watkins Glen, New York

Inaugural year: 1986 (most recent)

Race date: August

Size of track: 2.45 miles road course

Shopping potential: 3

Who's hot: Jeff Gordon, Tony Stewart, Kevin Harvick, Robby Gordon

Strutting Your Stuff

Okay, ladies, if you have made it this far, you are definitely on the right track. Playing and looking the part of a driver's wife or girlfriend is not about what everyone else expects; it is about you being you but in a high-profile kind of way. Let's face it, when you date or marry a NASCAR driver your private life becomes not so private, especially on race day. If you feel like everyone is watching you—they probably are.

So how is one to handle living life under a microscope? It can be tough at times, but there are a few tips that can help you manage.

Tips to Surviving the High-Profile Lens
1. Stay true to who you are regardless of what others say or do.
2. Remember there is nothing anyone can say about you that will change who you are.
3. Reach out to develop friendships. Having friends at the track is an essential tool to surviving the hectic racer's lifestyle. No one understands the life of a racer's wife like a racer's wife.
4. Keep a low profile on race day.
5. Do not grant interviews to the media during race weekends.

The Top Five . . .
MOST RECOGNIZABLE SIGNIFICANT OTHERS
1. DeLana Harvick, wife of Kevin Harvick
2. Chandra Johnson, wife of Jimmie Johnson
3. Buffy Waltrip, wife of Michael Waltrip
4. Nicole Lunders, longtime girlfriend of Greg Biffle
5. Kim Burton, wife of Jeff Burton

6. Mind what you say about your guy, his team, someone else's team, another driver, or his significant other. You never know who might turn your innocent comments into something negative.

7. Always abide by the racers' golden rule . . . Hear no evil, see no evil, and speak no evil!

Styling and Profiling

Rolling out the red carpet and dressing to the nines is not something you see often in the NASCAR Nextel Cup Series, but it does happen. There are a few "just can't miss" events each year that every girl wishes she could attend with her favorite driver. When it comes down to it, only a lucky few get to go arm in arm with the guy of their dreams. If you make it on your guy's guest list for these events, sister, you are on the right track.

High-Profile Events

1. **NASCAR Nextel Cup Series Awards Banquet.** This annual event is held at the historic Waldorf-Astoria hotel in New York City. The Awards Banquet is where the series champion is crowned and the top ten drivers in points receive their big checks. The eleventh-place finisher in points, the Rookie of the Year, and the most popular Driver of the Year (which is usually Dale Earnhardt Jr.) are also recognized. The event is usually scheduled the first weekend of December and is broadcast live on television.

2. **Daytona 500.** The granddaddy of all stock car racing, this race marks the beginning of a new race season, serving as the NASCAR Nextel Cup

Girlfriend to Girlfriend

Whoever the single driver takes to the banquet is crowned their date of the year. Usually only serious dating material makes it this far. If the driver does not have a serious girlfriend or does not feel the urge to ask anyone they have dated, they will usually ask a family member (like a sister or mother) or just fly solo.

Girlfriend to Girlfriend

*T*he ladies love the trip to the Awards Banquet due to the shopping and Broadway shows. There are few places as magical during the Christmas season as New York. The popular Rockefeller Center Christmas tree lighting usually takes place the same weekend.

Did You Know. . .

The Daytona 500 ends a two-week stay in Daytona. The teams pull into Daytona early February for practice, qualifying, and the nonpoints Budweiser Shootout event.

Series opener. Held mid-February at the beautiful Daytona International Speedway, more media cover this stock car race event than any other. It is very exciting to be in Daytona for Speedweeks. This is a fun event to go to not only due to the atmosphere of the speedway itself but the whole Daytona experience: from the beaches, to the shopping and restaurants, and all the extra events going on. Even after all of my years in the sport, my heart still races when I arrive in Daytona for Speedweeks.

3. **Allstate 400 at the Brickyard.** While the Daytona 500 receives more media hype and buzz than any other NASCAR Nextel Cup Series race, the Allstate 400 at the Indianapolis Motor Speedway, aka the Brickyard, certainly runs a close second. Even though the NASCAR Nextel Cup Series has only been running on this track since 1994, the track itself has been in existence since 1909. Winning at the Brickyard is one of the most prestigious achievements a driver can list on his racing résumé.

4. **NASCAR Nextel All-Star Challenge.** Held annually at the Lowe's Motor Speedway in Charlotte, this race runs the week prior to the Coca-Cola 600, which gives the teams (a hard-to-find) two weeks at home. The invitation-only race field is made up of drivers who have won races in either the same season of the event, or the full season prior. It is also open to past champions of the event, the NEXTEL Open winner (a race held immediately before the race for all drivers not eligible by wins), and the driver voted in by the fans.

5. **Ford 400 at Homestead-Miami.** The last event of the NASCAR Nextel Cup Series annual schedule. This race creates a media frenzy every year due to the fact that the series champion is not usually decided until the closing laps.

How They Met

Buffy and Michael Waltrip

Michael Waltrip is no ordinary guy. Some fellow competitors swear his second profession should be stand-up comedian. Being the nonconventional guy that he is, when the time came to pop the question to his girlfriend, Elizabeth (Buffy) Franks, he decided to make it something (or somewhere) neither she nor the racing world would soon forget.

Michael was so overcome with joy and emotion after winning the April 1993 NASCAR Busch Series race at Bristol that he announced in a Victory Lane television interview that he would marry Buffy one day. Reporter Benny Parsons asked Michael if that was a proposal. Michael turned around to Buffy and asked her to be his wife. While millions of fans watched, Buffy said yes. Michael and Buffy were married at the end of that race season.

The couple first crossed paths while she was attending the University of North Carolina and working as a part-time waitress at a popular driver hangout in the Charlotte area. Michael would come into the restaurant several times a week, but she did not know who he was at first. They struck up a friendship, but nothing more, as she was busy living the college life and he was already racing, which kept him away from home quite a bit.

After she graduated from college, she was hired by Sports Image, a company that produced and distributed licensed NASCAR driver apparel. Her position with the company also put her on the road following the NASCAR Busch and Cup Series events, which brought her and Michael together almost every weekend. The two would hang out, but were nothing more than good friends until a racing-related accident in August 1992 changed the way they felt about each other.

Buffy received a call that Michael was involved in a wreck during the Michigan race that sent him to a nearby hospital in Jackson. It was during the hours spent at the hospital that she and Michael realized their feelings had changed. From then on what started out as a friendship blossomed into a full-blown love story.

Dressing the Part

S potting a NASCAR Nextel Cup Series driver's wife or girlfriend on race day is usually not that difficult. In a world filled with uniformed men running around with tires and wrenches in their hands, beautiful ladies dressed in anything other than a uniform (unless you are DeLana Harvick) tend to stand out.

Drivers' significant others usually do not appear on race day until right before the MRO church service, which is held a few hours before the start of the race. They stay through the start of the race, then most of them go to the pits while the others choose to watch the race from the motor coaches.

The two most visible times for a driver's wife are drivers' introduction and Victory Lane. Drivers' introduction is certainly the most who's-who moment of any given race weekend. It is also a fashion show of sorts, with outfits ranging from jeans to suits, and everything in between. Most of the wives wear dress pants with nice blouses and high heel shoes. Now I am not talking three-inch stilettos, but they're not flats either. Some ladies can take dressing-up to extremes, but most find a nice balance between fashion and comfort.

Every woman has her own sense of style and a way in which she chooses to present herself. Drivers' wives make up a vast array of those styles from cutesy Girl Next Door to bold Runway Chic. Which sense of style best describes you?

Girl Next Door
Colors: Pink, purple, white, lime green
Style: Youthful

Favorite item: Hair clips

Favorite stores: Old Navy, Betsey Johnson, Target, Claire's

Sexy Siren
Colors: Red, pink, black, white
Style: Seductive
Favorite item: Anything that shows what you've got
Favorite stores: Victoria's Secret, bebe, The Limited, Candies

American Pie
Colors: Blue, green, burgundy, khaki
Style: Understated
Favorite item: Jeans
Favorite stores: The Gap, J. Crew, Abercombie & Fitch, Tommy Hilfinger

Nature Gal
Colors: Olive, khaki, navy, ivory
Style: Comfortable
Favorite item: Cargo pants
Favorite stores: Eddie Bauer, Lands' End, Coldwater Creek, REI

The Classic
Colors: Black, gray, navy, brown
Style: Timeless
Favorite item: Little black dress
Favorite stores: Ann Taylor, Banana Republic, Talbots, Brooks Brothers, J. Jill

Runway Chic
Colors: Black, this season's "new black"
Style: High-fashion
Favorite item: Anything that's ahead of the curve
Favorite stores: H&M, TJ Maxx, Lord & Taylor, Nordstrom

Girlfriend to Girlfriend

Many drivers' girlfriends come into the sport dressing one way, but by the time they become a serious significant other, they change their race day style. Most of the ladies take their appearance on race day very seriously—as one would expect, with a mere several million viewers watching.

The Top Five . . .
BEST-DRESSED WIVES

1. Eva Busch, wife of Kurt Busch
2. Buffy Waltrip, wife of Michael Waltrip
3. Kim Burton, wife of Jeff Burton
4. Donna Labonte, wife of Bobby Labonte
5. Shana Mayfield, wife of Jeremy Mayfield

Once you determine your style, see which driver fits you:

Girl Next Door—Kyle Busch, Jon Wood

Sexy Siren—Dale Earnhardt Jr., Paul Menard, Jamie McMurray, Martin Truex Jr.

American Pie—Greg Biffle, Denny Hamlin, Reed Sorenson, Brian Vickers, David Stremme

Nature Gal—Carl Edwards, Elliott Sadler

The Classic—Clint Bowyer, Kasey Kahne, Tony Stewart

Runway Chic—Robby Gordon, Casey Mears

Best Face Forward

Have you ever looked at someone and thought, "Wow I love that outfit, but what is wrong with her hair?" Looking good is not just about what you wear, it's about the whole you. Having a great haircut and wearing flattering makeup are the things that sometimes we girls let fall to the wayside. Strutting your stuff is all about attitude. Knowing that you look good from head to toe makes people stop in their tracks and say "now that is a put-together girl."

Racetrack Beauty Secrets

1. **Always, always, always wear sunscreen.** Spending countless hours at a racetrack will take a toll on your skin. Tip: Look for foundations with SPF.

2. **Spritz your skin a few times a day while sitting outdoors.** This will keep you cool and your skin moisturized. Spritzing also keeps you looking dewy fresh.

3. **Consider wearing a stylish hat on really bright sunny days to shade your face from the sun.** Ashley Judd (who is married to Indy racer Dario Franchitti) sports many different hats on race day to keep that flawless complexion.

4. **Drink lots of water during the day.** This not only keeps you hydrated, but your skin as well.

5. **An apple a day keeps the cellulite away.** Eating junk food while sitting for hours on end watching a race is not good for the bottom side.

6. **Less makeup is more.** Think Tammy Faye in 95 degrees. Going lighter on the makeup in hot, humid temperatures is not only smart but highly recommended. The last thing you want to do is end up on camera with your mascara making a pit stop on your cheeks.

7. **Wear shades.** Sporting shades at the track will protect your eyes from the outside glare as well as protect your face from the future . . . can you say crow's-feet?

Girlfriend to Girlfriend

One of my favorite beauty items is DuWop Lip Venom. It goes on like lip gloss but it naturally plumps up your lips. It also has a refreshing taste of cinnamon. I love to put it on underneath my favorite lipstick.

Track Smack Lip Attack

With over one million different lip colors out there to choose from, there is a little something for everyone. One day you may feel a little peachy, the next maybe fire engine red. Whatever your mood may be, when the cameras are rolling you want to make sure your lips are race ready.

Top Track Smackers

Best peach—Dior Addict Ultra Shine Sheer Lip color in Shiniest Flirt
Best pink—Tarte Lipstick in Darling
Best red—Vincent Longo Velvet Riche Rejuvenating Lipstick in Ignition
Best coral—Clinique Color Surge Lipstick in Coral Crush
Best rose—Dior Addict Lipstick in Rose Scenario
Best glosses—Nars Lip Gloss in Stolen Kisses, Cargo Lip Gloss Duo's in Soho and Okeechobee

Girlfriend to Girlfriend

Gum is a big *NO-NO* in public. There is nothing worse than seeing someone chew gum when the cameras are rolling.

The Purse Factor—Every Girl's Tool Chest

What to carry in your purse on race day should be considered part of your race day strategy. Expo Row may offer everything one's heart desires in racing merchandise, but don't think you are going to find a Lancôme makeup counter. Planning ahead will advance you way beyond your competition, so take notes.

The Must Haves

- Breath mints—no gum!
- Dental floss
- Lipstick with SPF
- Hand sanitizer
- Cash
- Travel toothbrush and toothpaste
- Hand cream
- Sunscreen
- Brush
- Granola bar
- Travel-size perfume
- Feminine products—just in case
- Cell phone
- Advil/Tylenol
- Tissues

The Top Five . . .

SCENTS TO HIS HEART

1. Lucky Number 6
2. Lovely Liquid Satin
3. Donna Karan Gold
4. Victoria's Secret Heavenly
5. L'Occitane Vanilla

Potty Time

Finding the time for a bathroom break on race day is a big challenge, especially when it comes to finding one without a mile-long line. How can something so simple require so much planning? If you are watching the race from the motor coach then your potty break problems are solved, but if you want to be where the action is, mapping out your quick exit is a must.

Portable bathrooms are lined up and down pit road, but I would venture to say that a driver's wife or girlfriend would not want to be caught dead in one, even though they are the most convenient. Designating your pit stop stall for the day does not have to be difficult; just well thought out. Remember, the most successful race teams plan ahead.

Davey was leading a race at Darlington one year when I realized that my bladder could not withstand another minute. Out of desperation, I quickly slipped into the Porta Potti closest to our pit stall. Not only was it one of the grossest experiences of my life, but a photographer (who somehow thought my potty break was more interesting than the race itself) snapped a picture of me exiting the potty hellhole, complete with toilet paper trailing behind. Trust me when I say . . . skip the Porta Potti temptation!

Potty Stop Strategies

As a driver's date or girlfriend:

1. Use the restroom before you leave the motor coach.
2. Know where to find the restrooms in the garage areas.
3. If the walk is not too far, venture back to the motor coach.
4. Always carry hand sanitizer.
5. Stash a little extra toilet paper in your purse.

When watching from the grandstands (still working on that first date):

1. Map out the closest restroom to your seat.
2. Use the restroom before you ever sit in your seat.
3. When the caution comes out, run (don't walk) to the bathroom, as most people will wait to see what happened on the track before they leave their seat.
4. Always carry hand sanitizer and extra toilet paper.
5. If all else fails, scream "Omigosh, it's Junior!" and watch the bathroom empty out.

Now, Let the Party Begin

Victory Lane is the greatest place on the face of the earth for a racer. This is the place that every NASCAR Nextel Cup Series driver strives to visit over and over again. The more they win . . . the more they want to win.

Victory Lane is a time for a driver to celebrate with his team but it is also a time for the car owner, sponsors, family, friends, and significant other to join in the celebration. Every driver is different in how they handle Victory Lane with their significant other. Usually, a driver climbs out of his car, quickly addresses the media, then immediately turns to his wife or girlfriend for a congratulatory kiss, but this is not always the case.

The single drivers are not as apt to show off their girlfriends to the NASCAR fans and media, which can make their significant other (even if only for the day) feel hung out to dry.

When starting out as a driver's date or even girlfriend, taking the slow route is the better option. Play it safe by leaving it up to your racer when to make his moves and how he wants you perceived by his fans and media alike. Once you get past the initial stages of dating, you will find your happy place (and face) in Victory Lane. Until then, sit back and enjoy the party.

The Top Five . . .

BEST HAIR

1. Carl Edwards
2. Kasey Kahne
3. David Stremme
4. Paul Menard
5. Robby Gordon

How to Act When the Cameras Are Rolling

The last thing a driver's wife wants to be known as is a camera hound! Some drivers' wives go to great lengths to keep themselves far from the camera lens, while others do everything they can to be in the line of fire. The best-kept secret is to go about your race day as normal but always remember you never know when the cameras may be on you. In live television, a quick shot might be the very minute you decided to pick your teeth.

You Might Be a Camera Hound If:
- You are on a first-name basis with every pit reporter.
- Your name is listed in the race day coverage credits.
- You kiss your guy while he is giving his live winner's network interview.
- You advise the TV camera crew where you will be during the race.
- You are not sure who won the race, but you are sure you got on camera at least once.
- In the racing archives there is not a single picture of your guy without you in it.

You Might Be a Low-Profiler If:
- You wait until the live network interview from Victory Lane is complete before you plant a big one on your guy's lips.
- You graciously step aside while the crew and sponsors take pictures with your man in Victory Lane.
- You watch the race from inside your motor coach to ensure more privacy.
- You do not grant interviews.
- While sitting on the pit box you stay focused on the race rather than ensuring that the photographers get your best side.
- You step aside when the live film crew is attempting to get shots of the race team in action.

Celebrate!

NASCAR Nextel Cup Series wins are not only hard to come by but also (for most) few and far between. In September 2006, Jeff Burton ended a 175-race winless streak (the second longest in NASCAR Nextel Cup Series history) by capturing a win at Dover. Casey Mears, in his fifth full season, has yet to win a race.

Countless man-hours go into preparing race cars and putting teams in contention to win races. To underrate a win for a driver would be doing him and his team a huge injustice. If there was ever a reason to celebrate, it would be a NASCAR Nextel Cup Series win.

Happy Hour

Somehow (can't imagine why) Victory Lane and happy hour go hand in hand. Beer sponsors have been a part of NASCAR Nextel Cup Series racing for many years, but it wasn't until 2005 that NASCAR started allowing hard liquor to sponsor race cars. NASCAR was basically pushed in the corner by Cup Series car owners who were hoping to open the door to other primary sponsors. As the dollar amount for primary sponsors ($15 to

---

The Top Five . . .

WAYS TO CELEBRATE A WIN

1. Throw a party until the cows come home.
2. Invite the entire team over to his place for a cookout, but you do all the cooking (or call in a caterer).
3. Prepare his favorite meal and serve it by candlelight for just the two of you. The first toast is to his win and more to come.
4. Treat him to a night out at his favorite restaurant.
5. Invite his family for dinner, topped off with a personalized race cake recognizing his win.

$20 million annually) continues to rise, the number of companies who can afford primary sponsorship dwindles.

Currently in the NASCAR Nextel Cup Series beer and liquor companies are represented by top-level drivers who no doubt sell lots of product. The only thing the series is missing is wine.

A Beer-Drinking Woman . . .

- Is just one of the boys
- Can belch with the best of 'em
- Is down-to-earth
- Loves pickup trucks
- Loves Dale Earnhardt Jr.

A Liquor-Drinking Woman . . .

- Means business
- Can take you down in arm wrestling
- Is serious about her NASCAR
- Can drink you under the table
- Loves Tony Stewart

A Wine-Drinking Woman . . .

- Is reserved
- Prefers the suites to the grandstands
- Enjoys nice things
- Drives a BMW
- Loves Jeff Gordon

Girlfriend to Girlfriend

Most drivers' wives and girlfriends do not consume alcohol on race day. The only acceptable place for a significant other to partake alcohol would be in the privacy of a driver's motor coach. Racing is a big business and race day is when the rubber meets the road, which means the drivers are all business as are most of their wives and girlfriends.

fast fact

The final practice before the race is referred to as Happy Hour. Happy Hour usually occurs on the afternoon or evening the day prior to the race. Even though it is called Happy Hour, some final practices actually last up to two hours.

The Compatibility Test

Not everyone is cut out to be a racer's wife or even girlfriend. Take this test to see if you really are cut out for life in the fast lane.

1. **Are you willing to travel almost every weekend February through November?**
   A. Yes
   B. No
   C. Maybe

2. **Can you handle the fact that he will very seldom be at family functions?**
   A. Yes
   B. No
   C. Maybe

3. **Will you understand that he cannot take you out for a romantic dinner for your birthday because qualifying just so happens to be that night?**
   A. Yes
   B. No
   C. Maybe

4. **Is the fact that he missed your firstborn's kindergarten graduation really not a big deal?**
   A. Yes
   B. No
   C. Maybe

5. **Would you totally understand that your vacation had to be postponed because a rained-out race was rescheduled for that weekend?**
   A. Yes
   B. No
   C. Maybe

6. **Is it really okay that he had to cancel a date again because he was at the race shop discussing setups for this weekend's race?**
   A. Yes
   B. No
   C. Maybe

7. **Does the fact that the grass is five feet tall because he does not have time (again) to cut it not bother you?**
   A. Yes
   B. No
   C. Maybe

8. **Is it okay that he might not be able to get back in time for your baby's birth because he has to race to maintain the points lead in the NASCAR Nextel Cup?**
   A. Yes
   B. No
   C. Maybe

9. **Do you really not mind playing second fiddle on race day?**
   A. Yes
   B. No
   C. Maybe

10. **You understand that he is two hours late to your date because practice ran later than expected?**
   A. Yes
   B. No
   C. Maybe

Where you rate:

If you answered mainly As—You are one tough cookie and can stand by your NASCAR man without a problem.

If you answered mainly Bs—You might want to rethink your position.

If you answered mainly Cs—You probably have not found your Mr. Right.

Pit Road Wisdom

Reaching your final destination is not just about getting there, it's how you got there. Regardless of what road you take, all roads have left and right turns and a few bumps along the way. It's not just about finding your way; it's about not forgetting where you came from.

Part Seven

The Checkered Flag

On to Victory Lane!

Drivers' Wives Then and Now

Drivers' wives are a rare breed to say the very least, and come from all walks of life. Some grew up in racing while others had never seen a race car a day in their lives . . . at least not until they met their Mr. Right. The role current drivers' wives play in their husbands' careers is very different from what was the norm for drivers' wives many years ago.

Drivers' wives today are more visible and certainly more media savvy. This is due largely to the fact that drivers' wives were not allowed to accompany their husbands in the garage and pit areas until the mid 1970s. Before that time, NASCAR did not allow women in the "men only" area—it was supposedly too dangerous, and a place of work for men only.

Because of the NASCAR restrictions set in place for the drivers' wives, they were forced to either stay at home or watch the race from the grandstands (this is before the Drivers' Compound existed). In the early 1970s, some of the more gutsy wives started sneaking into the infield and garage area of the NASCAR sanctioned tracks, praying not to get caught or daring someone to ask them to leave.

NASCAR took note and started allowing women in the restricted areas. It was during that time that the wives started playing a more active role in their husbands' careers. Stevie Waltrip, the wife of Darrell Waltrip, was one of the most visible wives. She was al-

Girlfriend to Girlfriend

Drivers' wives are tough women that have extremely thick skin. I did a lot of growing up my first year as a driver's wife. The lessons I learned from my years sitting atop a pit box and the relationships I cultivated have served me well.

ways referred to as the redhead on the pit box. Stevie turned every lap of DW's career from atop a pit box. She reminded Darrell when he retired that she retired too, which is all too true.

Some drivers' wives choose to sit in the pits to do what Stevie did for many years, while others are more comfortable staying in their motorcoaches, out of the limelight. Some wives have a hand in everything that goes on in their husbands' careers, while others choose not to know. The one common de-nominator is they all fell in love with a guy that just happens to drive race cars for a living.

Going to the Chapel

Each driver's wife has her own story of how she met her Mr. Right. Some have known their husbands since they were kids, while others only knew their husbands a short time before they tied the knot. Whatever the case, they all knew early on that their only competition was a 3,400-pound beauty with four tires.

Judy Allison

Husband: Bobby Allison, 1983 NASCAR Winston Cup champion
Children: Davey, Clifford, Bonnie, and Carrie
Proposed: He popped the question after her beautician school graduation dinner
Married: 1960
Years in racing: 50

WHAT YOU NEED TO KNOW

- One of the first members of the Racing Wives Auxiliary
- Bobby and Judy lost two sons in less than a year, one in a racing accident and one in a helicopter crash
- The two divorced in 1995 and remarried in 2000

Kim Burton

Husband: Jeff Burton
Children: Kimberle, Harrison

Proposed: On a date in their hometown
Married: February 1, 1992
Honeymoon: Cancun
Years in racing: 15+

WHAT YOU NEED TO KNOW

- Met Jeff when she was only fourteen years old
- Kim and Jeff were high school sweethearts
- Kim holds a degree in math and science education
- Taught school before Jeff went full-time Cup racing
- Sits atop Jeff's pit box for every race

Eva Busch

Husband: Kurt Busch, 2004 NASCAR Nextel Cup Series champion
Children: None
Proposed: July 27, 2005, in Prague, Czech Republic
Married: July 27, 2006 in Eastville, Virginia
Years in Racing: 3

WHAT YOU NEED TO KNOW

- Kurt and Eva met on a blind date at a sports bar in Charlotte
- Eva was told that she was being set up with a veterinarian
- Kurt, being old-fashioned at heart, asked Eva's dad for permission to marry his daughter
- Eva arrived at her wedding in a horse-drawn Cinderella carriage

you might be a nascar wife if . . .

- You throw the black flag at your husband for taking too long in the bathroom.
- You agree that Darlington Raceway is a great place for a honeymoon.
- You tell the kids to look both ways for race cars.
- You sleep better with the roar of the engines.
- Cleaning house consists of cleaning the rims of your motor coach.

- Worked as a customer service rep for a bank when they met
- Currently serves as vice president of Kurt's racing company

Cindy Elliott

Husband: Bill Elliott, 1988 NASCAR Winston Cup champion
Children: Chase
Proposed: In a casual conversation after dinner one night and reminded her the next day that he was serious
Married: December 12, 1992
Years in racing: 18+

WHAT YOU SHOULD KNOW:
- Met while Cindy was a photographer for *Winston Cup Scene*
- Quit her job after getting engaged to Bill
- Considers photography a passion
- Cindy and Bill's son, Chase, wants to race just like his dad

DeLana Harvick

Husband: Kevin Harvick
Children: None
Proposed: After running out for a Wendy's Frosty
Married: February 28, 2001
Honeymoon: Las Vegas
Years in racing: Entire life

WHAT YOU NEED TO KNOW
- Grew up at racetracks, as her father was a racer
- Raced Late Models at a local track in Kenly, North Carolina
- Met Kevin while working as a PR rep
- Wears a full team uniform for Cup Series races
- Serves as president of Kevin Harvick, Incorporated

Chandra Johnson

Husband: Jimmie Johnson
Children: None
Proposed: On a mountaintop in Beaver Creek, Colorado, in 2003
Married: December 11, 2004

Honeymoon: St. Barts on Rick Hendrick's 150-foot yacht

Years in racing: 5

WHAT YOU NEED TO KNOW

- Former professional Wilhelmina model
- Graduated from University of Oklahoma
- Introduced by Jeff Gordon in 2002
- Married in St. Barts, the location of their first vacation together

Katie Kenseth

Husband: Matt Kenseth, 2003 NASCAR Nextel Cup Series champion

Children: Ross (stepson)

Married: December 4, 2000

Honeymoon: Caribbean

Years in racing: 8+

WHAT YOU NEED TO KNOW

- Matt and Katie met at a mutual friend's wedding
- Both are Cambridge, Wisconsin, natives
- Katie is one of the most private wives on the circuit
- Considers Krissie Newman one of her closest friends

Donna Labonte

Husband: Bobby Labonte, 2000 NASCAR Nextel Cup Series champion

Children: Robert, Madison

Proposed: October 1990

Married: Easter weekend 1991

Honeymoon: Hickory Motor Speedway, Hickory, North Carolina

Years in racing: 20+

WHAT YOU NEED TO KNOW

- Donna met Bobby while she was working at Revco
- Believes in love at first sight
- Graduated from Guilford Technical Community College in 1986
- Dated for eight years before becoming engaged

Paula Marlin

Husband: Sterling Marlin
Children: Steadman, Sutherlin
Proposed: Christmas Day 1977
Married: July 1978
Years in racing: 25+

WHAT YOU NEED TO KNOW

- Paula and Sterling met on a double date (each with someone else)
- Married right out of high school
- Paula and Sterling are soon to celebrate their thirtieth wedding anniversary
- Paula is known for her cooking
- Paula's nickname is Miss Paula

Arlene Martin

Husband: Mark Martin
Children: Amy, Rachel, Heather, Stacy, Matt
Proposed: August 1984
Married: October 27, 1984
Years in racing: 20+

WHAT YOU NEED TO KNOW

- Arlene was a divorced mother of four when she met Mark
- Arlene and Mark were set up on a blind date by Mark's sister, Glenda
- Arlene and Mark's son, Matt, hopes to be the next-generation Martin driver
- Arlene and Mark broke the unspoken NASCAR driver rule by choosing to live in Daytona Beach and not the Charlotte area

The Top Five . . .

NAMES FOR A NASCAR DRIVER'S FIRSTBORN

1. Chase
2. Rider
3. Daytona
4. Ricky Bobby
5. Champion

Shana Mayfield

Husband: Jeremy Mayfield
Children: None
Married: June 4, 2003
Honeymoon: Turks and Caicos
Years in racing: 7+

WHAT YOU NEED TO KNOW

- Graduated from Clemson University
- Once considered a job in sports marketing
- Shana and Jeremy met at Darlington Raceway in 1999
- Married in Myrtle Beach, South Carolina

Andrea Nemechek

Husband: Joe Nemechek
Children: John, Blair, Kennedy
Proposed: March 1990
Married: November 21, 1992
Years in racing: 18+

WHAT YOU NEED TO KNOW

- Grew up in Myrtle Beach, South Carolina
- Graduated from University of South Carolina with a degree in retail management in 1988
- Andrea's father suggested numerous times that Andrea meet his good friend's son Joe before they ever met
- Andrea met Joe at a charity event

Did You Know...

While the France family is the first family of NASCAR, many believe the names Earnhardt and Petty are more recognizable.

Krissie Newman

Husband: Ryan Newman
Children: None
Married: January 3, 2004
Honeymoon: Jackson Hole, Wyoming
Years in racing: 5+

WHAT YOU NEED TO KNOW

- Met in 2001
- Set up on a date by her grandmother
- Worked as a clerk for a North Carolina judge
- Spearheaded the NASCAR *Pit Road Pets* book project
- Animal activist
- Rescued animals from the New Orleans hurricane disaster

Lynda Petty

Husband: Richard Petty, seven-time NASCAR Nextel Cup Series champion
Children: Kyle, Sharon, Lisa, Rebecca
Proposed: In a casual conversation Richard suggested they get married
Married: Summer 1959
Years in racing: 50+

How They Met

LYNDA AND RICHARD PETTY

Lynda Owens was a carefree fourteen-year-old when she met the tall, lanky nineteen-year-old son of the famous racer Lee Petty. They both had been in Randleman, North Carolina, their entire lives but had never crossed paths before. That is, not until her best friend started dating Richard's brother, Maurice, and Richard and Lynda were thrown together. Luckily, the two found that they enjoyed each other's company and became friends. What started out as a casual friendship turned into a full-blown relationship before either could figure out what was going on; their feelings for each other surprised them both.

Richard, who was not racing yet, had been around racing all his life, but Lynda had not and knew very little about the sport. She tried to understand the crazy passion the Petty family had for racing but she didn't always get it. In July of 1958, Richard decided it was his turn to get behind the wheel of a race car, which is what started the illustrious career of the King.

The distance between Richard and Lynda (due to his hectic racing schedule) got to be too much for Richard, which is what brought him to the unexpected "Let's get married" comment he made to her on one of his trips back home. As with most racing couples, Richard and Lynda wasted little time getting to the chapel. In fact, they were so excited and ready to get married that they didn't tell anyone of their plans. They took off for Chesterfield, South Carolina, to elope. After getting hitched, the two went back home to announce their marriage to their families. After the initial shock, both families embraced the news and celebrated with the newlywed couple.

WHAT YOU NEED TO KNOW

- Met Richard when she was only fourteen
- Has been married to the King of Stock Car Racing for fifty years
- One of the most beloved and respected drivers' wives
- Collects dolls

Pattie Petty

Husband: Kyle Petty

Children: Adam, Austin, Montgomery

Proposed: July 1978

Married: February 4, 1979

Years in racing: 30+

WHAT YOU NEED TO KNOW

- Met when Pattie was in college while Kyle was in high school
- Pattie attended Appalachian State University
- Pattie is a former Miss Winston
- Pattie and Kyle are founders of the Victory Junction Gang Camp

Ann Schrader

Husband: Kenny Schrader

Children: Dorothy, Sheldon

Proposed: She gave him a calendar and told him to pick a day

Married: November 13, 1984

Honeymoon: She went to work and he went racing

Years in racing: 25+

WHAT YOU NEED TO KNOW

- Ann and Kenny met while each were married to someone else
- Ann and her first husband were best friends with Kenny and his first wife
- Ann worked as a registered nurse in the early years of their marriage
- Ann was instrumental in the medical liaison position created by NASCAR
- Ann is known for her bubbly personality and her positive mind-set

Buffy Waltrip

Husband: Michael Waltrip

Children: Caitlin, Margaret "Macy"

Proposed: April 3, 1993
Married: November 27, 1993
Years in racing: 10+

What you need to know

- Buffy's given name is Elizabeth
- Met Michael while she was a waitress at a restaurant he frequented
- Graduated from University of North Carolina
- Worked for a NASCAR licensed driver apparel company after college

How Do You Measure Up as a Driver's Wife?

Being a driver's wife is not all that it is cut out to be. The life of a driver's wife is like a road course in that it is fast with many left and right turns. To stay on pace and on the lead lap, drivers' wives have to stay on their toes. They also have to wear many hats as they deal with media, sponsors, and even fans . . . not to mention highly competitive race car drivers and the up-and-down nature of the business. So, you still think you are cut out for it? Go ahead and fire your engine and see where you rank in the drivers' wives points system.

1. **Your guy just nailed another driver on the track for no apparent reason.**
   A. You hop on the radio to tell him how stupid that was.
   B. You ask him what happened as soon as the race is over.
   C. You wait for him to bring it up after the race and provide a listening ear.

2. **Your guy's sponsor just told you that your husband needs to get some wins.**
   A. You tell him to get a life and go take a hike.
   B. You say you'll talk to your husband about it.
   C. You calmly walk away and let your guy handle it.

3. **You are asked by a TV station to allow cameras in your motor coach for the last ten laps of the final race of the season and your guy is sitting in the top seat.**

A. You invite them in for tea and coffee to watch the race.

B. You agree to a brief interview right after the race.

C. You politely pass, as this is an emotional and stressful time.

4. **NASCAR asks you to head up a fund-raising effort for the Victory Junction Gang Camp.**

A. You tell them you are too busy racing but maybe next time.

B. You agree to help out at the event, but tell them you don't have time to be in charge.

C. You graciously accept because it is your duty to help give back to the racing community that has given you and your guy so much.

5. **You are standing in line for the restroom at the track but realize the line is moving slowly and you want to get back to the race.**

A. You tell everyone who you are and expect to be moved up in line.

B. You decide to run back to your motor coach, even if it will probably take longer than staying where you are.

C. You wait your turn just like everybody else.

6. **It has been a long day at the track and you are more than ready to go, but a group of fans who have been waiting for an hour to see your guy are standing near your car.**

A. You insist your guy get in his car and head to the airport without acknowledging the fans who have been waiting.

B. You ask your guy if he could just sign a few autographs this time.

C. You wait patiently while your guy takes the time to meet and greet each of his fans.

7. **Another driver's wife you don't know well asks you and your guy to a cookout after practice.**

A. You snub your nose and go about your business.

B. You tell her maybe, and wait until after practice to decide if you feel up to going.

C. You graciously accept and ask what you can bring.

8. **A media rep asks you to comment on a race situation.**

A. You tell him exactly what you think about it.

B. You make a few carefully chosen comments.

C. You politely pass on the opportunity.

Did You Know. . .

Most drivers' wives feel it's a faux pas to ask for another driver's autograph, even for a friend.

Girlfriend to Girlfriend

Some of the most important relationships drivers' wives have are with each other. Few people can understand the life of a racing wife. In this case it certainly almost always takes one to know one. Some of my closest friends in life have come from roots planted many years ago in the garage area.

9. **Your guy asks you to bring his lunch to the hauler because he does not have time to get something to eat before the start of the race.**
    A. You tell him you are busy getting ready for the race too and he will have to get it himself.
    B. You pick up a burger and fries, and drop it off—not having time to stay.
    C. You fix his favorite pre-race lunch and enjoy a few minutes with him before the start of the race.

10. **A good friend asks you to get an autograph for her from another driver.**
    A. You go knocking on the other driver's motor coach and ask for an autograph for your friend.
    B. You say you'll try, and will only ask if you happen to run into the driver and it's convenient.
    C. You politely tell her that you are not comfortable with her request and leave it alone.

WHERE DO YOU RANK

As—5 points

Bs—7 points

Cs—10 points

100 points—You are championship material!

80 points—You finish the season in the top ten in points.

70 points or under—You might want to put in another practice lap or two.

NASCAR Trivia— Lovebird-Style

1. What NASCAR Nextel Cup Series driver's wife is nicknamed Buffy?

2. What former Miss Winston met her husband at the Fairgrounds Speedway in Nashville, Tennessee, before he made it to the big-time in NASCAR Nextel Cup Series racing?

3. What NASCAR Nextel Cup Series driver met his wife when she was only fourteen years old while she was out for an afternoon ride on her bicycle?

4. What driver's wife once worked as a staff photographer for *Winston Cup Scene*?

5. What driver's wife met her husband at Michigan International Speedway in 1999 while she was working as a public relations representative?

6. What NASCAR Nextel Cup Series veteran met his wife when she was seventeen years old while she was working as a clerk at the Revco Pharmacy in Thomasville, North Carolina?

7. What driver's wife met her husband after her boyfriend at the time set her cousin up with him (the driver) but he decided he had eyes for her and not the cousin?

8. What young, divorced, single mom of four girls met her husband in 1983 on a blind date that was set up by his sister?

9. What NASCAR Nextel Cup Series driver met his wife at a charity ball in Orlando, Florida, after her father introduced the two?

10. What NASCAR Nextel Cup racing legend has been married to his wife for over forty-five years?

11. What NASCAR Nextel Cup Series driver met his wife while they were both married to someone else?

12. What NASCAR Nextel Cup Series driver briefly dated veteran racer Rusty Wallace's daughter?

13. What NASCAR Nextel Cup Series driver married a former Wilhelmina model?

14. What NASCAR Nextel Cup Series driver briefly dated veteran racer Terry Labonte's daughter?

15. What NASCAR Nextel Cup Series driver has been dating his current girlfriend for over nine years?

16. What driver's wife and her husband are very active in animal rights?

17. What NASCAR Nextel Cup Series driver was introduced to his future wife as a veterinarian on a blind date in hopes of getting to know her without her realizing he was a famous race car driver?

18. What NASCAR on TNT analyst is married to a former race car driver?

19. What NASCAR Nextel Cup Series car owner met her husband through her uncle who was racing with her future husband at the time?

Answers

1. Michael Waltrip
2. Pattie Petty, wife of veteran racer Kyle Petty
3. Jeff Burton
4. Cindy Elliott, wife of veteran racer Bill Elliott
5. DeLana Harvick, wife of Kevin Harvick
6. Bobby Labonte
7. Paula Marlin, wife of Sterling Marlin
8. Arlene Martin, wife of Mark Martin
9. Joe Nemechek
10. The King, Richard Petty
11. Kenny Schrader
12. Jamie McMurray
13. Jimmie Johnson
14. Kasey Kahne
15. Greg Biffle
16. Krissie Newman, wife of Ryan Newman
17. Kurt Busch
18. Wally Dallenbach, married to the former Robin McCall
19. Teresa Earnhardt, widow of the late Dale Earnhardt, Sr., and niece of former Busch series racer Tommy Houston.

Pit Road Wisdom

Racing is racing and love is love. A racing career is short-lived, but love should last forever. When all is said and done on a driver's career, it is what's inside the helmet that makes him who he is. Seeing a driver as a driver is not seeing who they really are.

Appendix A

NASCAR Dictionary

Aerodynamics—The effect of air moving across, over, under, and around the race car.

Air pressure—The amount of forced air in a tire.

Alternator—A device mounted on the engine that keeps the battery charged while the engine is running. The alternator has a belt, referred to as the alternator belt.

Appearance—When a driver shows up at an event, such as a car lot, grand opening, or convention, to sign autographs and meet fans.

Apron—A portion of track that separates the racing section from the grass of the infield.

Associate sponsor—Companies who do not choose to or are not able to fund a primary sponsorship. They get less exposure for their dollar. A team can have many associate sponsors.

Autograph—A signature from someone famous.

Back stretch—The long straight portion of a racetrack located furthest from the grandstands.

Banking—The degree of angle on the track surface.

Bite/Round of bite—Adjusting or turning the jacking screws at each wheel. Simply put, it adds or reduces pressure on a large spring, which transfers weight from corner to corner of the car. Teams do this to help the tires stick to the track better.

Blocking—Keeping another driver from passing.

Body—The skin or metal covering of the car.

Camber—The amount of positive or negative angle the tire is from vertical.

Carburetor—An engine part that controls the air and fuel mixture supplied to the engine.

Car chief—The crew chief's right-hand man.

Champion—A driver who has won the NASCAR Cup Series title.

Chassis—The steel frame of the car.

Crankshaft—The car part that delivers power from the pistons to the transmission.

Crew chief—The race team boss.

Deck lid—The metal casing that covers the trunk of the car.

Donuts—The result of driving in a circular motion, leaving the shape of a donut on the track surface. Something a driver does when he wins a race.

Down force—The result of air flowing across the body of the car that presses it down on to the track.

Draft—The hole in the air made by the car. A car utilizing the draft runs in the hole in the air left by the car running in the front, thereby conserving gas and reducing stress on the engine.

Drafting—When cars race together to create faster speeds by taking advantage of aerodynamics.

Drag—The effect of the car going through the air. The less drag on the body of the car, the faster it will go.

Dyno—A machine used to measure an engine's horsepower.

Equalized tire—When the air pressure is the same in the inner and outer liner of a tire. An equalized tire causes a vibration felt by the driver.

Frame—The chassis of the race car.

Front stretch—The straight portion of the track surface located in front of the main grandstands and flag stand.

Fuel cell—Fuel tank.

Fuel pump—The car part that pumps fuel from the fuel cell to the carburetor.

Garage area—The secured area where the cars are kept and worked on throughout race weekend. You must have a special pass to enter the garage area.

Greenhouse—The structure that covers the upper area of a race car, which includes the area extending from the base of the windshield on the front of the car, across the tops of the doors, to the base of the window in the rear of the car.

Handling—How a car behaves on the track. If a driver has handling issues, his car does not race well.

Happy Hour—The last official practice before the start of the race.

Hauler—An eighteen-wheel tractor-trailer that transports the race cars from one track to another. Teams use the hauler as a meeting place on race weekends. This is where many tools and equipment are stored.

Horsepower—The amount of engine power a car has. Horsepower is measured by the amount of power it takes to move 33,000 pounds one foot in a minute.

Intermediate track—A racetrack that measures over a mile but less than two miles.

Interval—The distance between cars on the track. This is measured by car lengths or seconds.

Jet dryer—A machine used to dry the track surface quickly when Mother Nature rains down.

Lug nuts—Nuts used to attach the tire to the race car. The lug nuts are applied with a special air wrench during pit stops. Each tire has five lug nuts.

Marbles—Excess tire rubber found at the top of the racetrack.

Modern era—NASCAR's modern era dates from 1972 to the present.

Paint scheme—The artwork on a race car. Some drivers have special paint schemes for special events.

Pit box—A cabinet on wheels containing tools used by the pit crew, and computerized equipment to determine track speeds, tire wear, and gas mileage during the race.

Pit pass—A pass that allows the pass holder to enter the pit stall areas. A pre-race pit pass allows the pass holder to tour pit road before the start of the race. A Hot Pass allows the pass holder to stay in the pit during the race event.

Pit road—The road where pit crews service their cars.

Pit stall—The designated area for each team to service its car.

Pit stop—When a car enters pit road and comes to a stop in its specific pit stall for the team to service the car.

Pit wall—The wall that separates the pit stall area from pit road.

Pit window—An estimated number of laps a team feels their driver can run before coming in for a pit stop. This changes at every track due to track size.

Pole position—The number one starting spot; the fastest qualifier.

Primary sponsor—The team's main sponsor; the most noticeable sponsor you see when you look at the car, also the one that pays the most.

Provisional—A spot that allows a driver to compete in a race when he did not qualify on time. This is awarded to past champions and top drivers in points.

Quarter panel—The metal on both sides of the race car from the rear bumper below the deck lid to over the wheel well.

Relief driver—A driver standing by to replace the original driver due to illness or injury. All relief drivers must be approved by NASCAR.

Restart—The starting of the race after a caution period.

Restrictor plate—A metal plate that restricts the airflow from the carburetor to the engine. Restricting the airflow slows down the speed of the car. Restrictor plates are used at Daytona and Talladega.

Road courses—Tracks that have left and right turns versus the normal turn-left mode of the non–road course tracks. Infineon and Watkins Glen are the Cup Series road course tracks.

Roll cage—The steel frame that surrounds a driver in the driver cockpit area. This cage protects the driver if the car should roll or flip as well as protects the driver from a side impact.

Roof flaps—Flaps that lie flat on the top of the car unless the car spins or moves in an abrupt manner. The flaps are designed to help keep the cars on the track from going airborne.

RPMs—Revolutions per minute; the speed an engine is turning.

Scanner—Radio-type instrument that allows the listener to pick up on radio conversations between the team and driver.

Scuffs—Tires that are not new but usually have not been used for more than five laps.

Setup—The way in which a car is mechanically set up to race and/or qualify.

Short track—Tracks that are less than one mile in length.

Show cars—In most cases, old race cars that are not used for competition anymore, and are now used for appearance events, corporate events, and so on. Each show car has a driver that transports the car from one event to another.

Silly season—A time during the season when rumors start escalating about where certain drivers will go (with what team) for the following season. This usually starts about halfway through the season.

Stickers—New tires; tires that have the manufacturer stickers still attached, meaning they've never been used.

Superspeedway—A track measuring more than one mile in distance.

Tachometer—An instrument in the race car to help drivers determine pit road speed by displaying the engine's RPMs. It is also used to optimally gear the car.

Transponder—A device used to send an electronic signal to wires buried in the race cars. The device monitors lap times and assists in electronically scoring the cars.

Trunk lid—The rear deck lid.

Venue—A place that houses an event, used in generic form. For example, Lowe's Motor Speedway is a racing venue.

Victory Lane—Where the winning driver and team go to celebrate their win.

Wedge—The cross weight adjustment of a race car. Basically, putting more weight on the wheel by compressing the spring.

Window net—A mesh net that covers the driver's window area.

Wind tunnel—A research facility used to study the effects of air on the car by simulating forces of air over and around the car like those encountered during normal racing situations.

Appendix B
NASCAR Slang

Battling for position—Two or more cars racing each other for a position on the track.

Behind the wall—Taking the race car off pit road to either the garage area or behind the pit wall.

Blowing an engine or blowing up—When an engine expires or will not work anymore . . . a car cannot go without a working engine.

Brake check—When a driver hits his brakes just enough to make the car behind him touch the brakes. The brake-checking car then hits the gas pedal in a quick fashion. *Remember, no brake lights!*

Brushing the wall or tapping the wall—When a driver slightly brushes against the wall, with little or no damage.

Bump draft—When a car running in the draft bumps the rear bumper of the car in front of him; a nudge. The bump is used to give the other car a little boost, although some drivers use the bump draft as a warning to the car on the receiving end to get moving.

Clean air—Air that does not have turbulence from other race cars. If a driver comments that his car runs better in clean air, he basically means his car performs better out front.

Cookie-cutter track—A track that is not unique; nothing special.

Develops a push—Same as tight, see "tight out."

Dirty air—A term used for turbulent air caused by fast-moving cars, which can be good or bad. Some drivers feel a particular car may run better in dirty air.

Gas-and-go—When a driver comes in for a pit stop to get gas but no tires.

Going a lap down—A car that is close to being lapped; not scored on the lead lap.

Green flag conditions—This means the track is ready to race—clean, no debris.

Hitting your marks—Visual marks a driver makes at a track to help him know when to accelerate, let off gas, or pass. Each driver has specific things they use for marks, such as the flag stand or a certain marking on a portion of the wall.

Hung out to dry—A driver who gets out of the racing line or draft and quickly loses position on the track.

Lapped traffic—Cars that are not on the lead lap and are usually much slower than the lead pack.

Lead pack—The lead cars running in a pack of cars.

Loose-in—When the rear of the car feels like it is not stable, that it feels loose or squirmy; a common complaint from the drivers.

On the lead lap—Cars scored on the lead lap; cars not laps down.

Out front—Racing at the front of the other cars, in the lead.

Race-ready—A car that is ready to race.

Racing groove—Where the drivers want to race on certain tracks. It is like the highway versus a side road. The high groove will take a driver closer to the outside wall, whereas the lower groove will be closer to the bottom end of the track. Some tracks have more than one groove. Tracks can change over time, a one-groove track can become a two-groove track.

Right off the truck—A race car that has no work or changes done to it before hitting the track. Drivers use this term when a car runs well but had no significant changes from the race shop to the track.

Round of wedge—An adjustment of the pressure on the rear springs of the tires.

Running wide open—Pushing the accelerator to the floor.

Seasoned track—A track that has years of racing on the surface; a mature track surface.

Splash of gas—When the gas man only gives the driver enough gas to finish the race. You see this happen at the end of a race when track position is crucial.

Stop-and-go—A penalty NASCAR hands out to drivers who speed on pit road. The driver must enter the pit stall during an unscheduled pit stop and come to a complete stop (one full second) before the NASCAR official will allow the car to exit pit road.

Tail of the longest line—This is when a driver is sent to the end of the longest line of cars for the restart of the race due to a penalty handed down by NASCAR.

Tight-out—A car feels tight when the front tires will not turn well, making it tough to hold the car in the turns; also, if the driver turns the wheel more than the front of the car actually turns in the corner.

Trading paint—When drivers show aggressive driving techniques toward one another; lots of bumping and banging. Basically, putting one car's paint on another's from close racing; rubbing is racing.

Appendix C

Most Common "Just Have to Know" Questions

1. Can drivers' wives (or girlfriends) go to the drivers' meeting?

The answer is a big bold NASCAR *no!* Only the driver, car owner, and crew chief are allowed to attend the meeting.

2. Can girlfriends watch the races from the pits?

Yes, if the girlfriend is properly credentialed, meaning that she has been issued a Hot Pass from NASCAR. A Hot Pass enables you to be in the pits when the track is hot.

3. How many of the single NASCAR drivers have girlfriends?

That number changes from week to week. Several of the guys have long-time girlfriends, like Greg Biffle, who has been dating his girlfriend, Nicole Lunders, for close to ten years. But for the most part, the guys are *unattached and single-minded.*

4. Are most of the drivers' wives involved in their husbands' racing careers?

Yes. NASCAR racing is a lifestyle not a job, which makes it more likely to have the entire family involved in the sport. Not all of the wives take a hands-on approach to the everyday nature of the sport, but most play a significant role in their husbands' careers in some way or another. DeLana Harvick (Kevin Harvick's wife) is the most hands-on driver's wife currently. She is actively involved in the business side of Kevin's Busch and Truck Series programs, as well as a huge supporter of Kevin in the NASCAR Nextel Cup Series.

Did You Know. . .

The drivers' meeting is mandatory for all drivers and is usually held two hours before the start of the race.

Did You Know. . .

The track is referred to as hot when racing is taking place on the track.

5. Are NASCAR drivers only interested in race cars?

Well, some would argue that to be the case, but NASCAR drivers do enjoy their time away from racing as well. No one would have married drivers if drivers never thought about anything else. The toughest part for the guys is finding the time to meet someone and then follow through with finding time for dating. But as we all know, *boys will be boys*, and if there's a will there's a way.

6. Who travels with the drivers each weekend to the races?

This differs from driver to driver, but in most cases they are accompanied each week by all of their team members, car owner, PR rep that handles all of the media, sponsor reps, motor coach driver, and personal friends. Some drivers have their parents travel on the circuit with them, even though they usually stay in a separate motor coach or in a nearby hotel. The mothers of Carl Edwards and Joe Nemechek are two of the most visible moms on the circuit. Carl Edwards's mom is so well known that she has appeared in commercials with him.

7. Why are there no women race car drivers?

There are many opinions why women have not (to this point) excelled in NASCAR racing. The biggest obstacle female racers have faced in years past is the lack of great equipment, meaning female racers have not been given the same opportunities as men from a mechanical standpoint. Few top-notch teams have been willing to gamble on female racers for different reasons. This unfortunate scenario has given female racers no choice but to race in less competitive equipment, which puts them at a disadvantage when it comes

fast fact

There have been a handful of female racers through the years but none have ever captured the checkered flag; few have even seen it at a distance. Sara Christian was the first female to ever race a NASCAR event way back in 1949. Janet Guthrie is probably the most notable female racer to come along. She made thirty-three starts between 1976 and 1980. She made history in February 1977 when she became the first woman to ever qualify for the Daytona 500.

to showing their abilities. The Danica Patrick mania in the Indy Series has certainly opened the eyes of NASCAR car owners and sponsors. The race is now on to see who can come up with the Danica Patrick of NASCAR.

8. Do the drivers hang out with the other drivers when they are not racing?

It depends on the driver, but for the most part drivers do have their buddies both on and off the track. Kevin Harvick and Clint Bowyer are great friends, as are Tony Stewart and Dale Earnhardt Jr. Drivers spend an enormous amount of time at the racetrack so friendships do blossom and surprisingly withstand the on-track competition that takes place week in and week out.

9. How about the wives and girlfriends? Are they friendly to one another?

Absolutely! The majority of the significant others have long since figured out that what happens on the racetrack, stays on the racetrack. In my eighteen years in the sport, I have only seen a few cases where wives (or girlfriends) became involved in on-track situations. This type of behavior is frowned upon by the other wives and will get you nowhere fast!

10. Do drivers travel with their pets?

Yes, many of the drivers take their pets to the races each weekend. Greg Biffle and Ryan Newman have both spearheaded different animal-friendly projects to raise funds and awareness for their four-legged friends.

Appendix D

Modern Era Champions, 1972–2006

1972—Richard Petty
1973—Benny Parsons
1974—Richard Petty
1975—Richard Petty
1976—Cale Yarborough
1977—Cale Yarborough
1978—Cale Yarborough
1979—Richard Petty
1980—Dale Earnhardt Sr.
1981—Darrell Waltrip
1982—Darrell Waltrip
1983—Bobby Allison
1984—Terry Labonte
1985—Darrell Waltrip
1986—Dale Earnhardt Sr.
1987—Dale Earnhardt Sr.
1988—Bill Elliott

1989—Rusty Wallace
1990—Dale Earnhardt Sr.
1991—Dale Earnhardt Sr.
1992—Alan Kulwicki
1993—Dale Earnhardt Sr.
1994—Dale Earnhardt Sr.
1995—Jeff Gordon
1996—Terry Labonte
1997—Jeff Gordon
1998—Jeff Gordon
1999—Dale Jarrett
2000—Bobby Labonte
2001—Jeff Gordon
2002—Tony Stewart
2003—Matt Kenseth
2004—Kurt Busch
2005—Tony Stewart
2006—Jimmie Johnson

Appendix E

Money Honey

THE ALL-TIME MONEY LEADERS

Driver	Amount
1. Jeff Gordon	$82,358,526
2. Mark Martin	$59,428,575
3. Tony Stewart	$57,269,018
4. Dale Jarrett	$56,993,389
5. Bobby Labonte	$50,639,719
6. Rusty Wallace	$49,741,326
7. Jeff Burton	$46,898,336
8. Jimmie Johnson	$44,134,716
9. Matt Kenseth	$43,134,716
10. Dale Earnhardt Jr.	$42,945,535
11. Dale Earnhardt	$41,742,384
12. Ricky Rudd	$40,696,133
13. Terry Labonte	$40,559,678
14. Sterling Marlin	$40,298,514
15. Bill Elliott	$38,860,357
16. Kurt Busch	$36,194,280
17. Michael Waltrip	$35,193,442
18. Kevin Harvick	$33,571,638
19. Ken Schrader	$32,422,853
20. Ryan Newman	$31,519,766

In Closing

This book was intended to be a fun and somewhat wacky way to approach meeting a NASCAR driver.

As with most things in life, meeting your one-and-only, make-your-heart-skip-a-beat Mr. Right is not as easy as walking this way, or talking that way. It is about two people coming together to enjoy, learn, and grow with one another.

Sometimes relationships work out and sometimes they do not. At the end of the day, who you are and what you represent are your greatest gifts. If he is not your Mr. Right, keep on keeping on.

So come on, girls, whether you're winning over a NASCAR driver's heart or, as my grandmother says, waiting for the next bus to come along, remember to let your spirit shine on! Go get 'em!

About the Author

Few women have covered the sport of auto racing at the level of LIZ ALLISON, and even fewer have seen the NASCAR life from a driver's wife's perspective and later (after her husband, Davey Allison, was tragically killed in 1993) as a member of the media covering the sport.

Liz's passion for racing is evident in her professional career, as she is a popular radio personality in Nashville, Tennessee, where her top-notch reporting has gained her the number one NASCAR show in Nashville. She has hosted such television shows as *Motoring Music City* and served as a pit reporter for TNT for the NASCAR Nextel and Busch Series events.

In 2006, the release of *The Girl's Guide to NASCAR* prompted her appearances on the *Today* show, *Fox & Friends*, *20/20*, ESPN's *Cold Pizza*, and CNBC's *Street Signs*, as well as interviews on over one hundred radio stations nationwide. Liz's media savvy has also landed her appearances on CNN, CNNSI, TNN, and ESPN *Hot List*.

In 2004, Liz became the first (and only) female to take a seat in the skybox as race day announcer and color analyst for the Nashville Super-speedway, which plays host to an Indy Racing League event, two NASCAR Busch Series races, and a NASCAR Craftsman Truck Series competition.

The Girl's Guide to Winning a NASCAR Driver is her fifth published book on the sport and she serves as a contributing author to numerous publications.

Liz has remarried and lives in Nashville with her husband, Ryan, and their three children. For more information on her upcoming titles visit her online at www.lizallison.com.